GREENE & GREENE

Design Elements
for the Workshop

GREENE & GREENE

Design Elements for the Workshop

Darrell Peart

Linden Publishing

Fresno

Greene and Greene: Design Elements for the Workshop

By Darrell Peart

© 2005 Darrell Peart

7986

All drawings by Darrell Peart

Photos by Darrell Peart unless otherwise noted

Cover design by James Goold

ISBN: 978-0-941936-96-5

ISBN: 0-941936-96-1

Printed in China

Library of Congress Cataloging -In-Publication information
Peart, Darrell, 1950-
    Greene and Greene : design elements for the workshop / by Darrell Peart.
        p. cm.
    Includes bibliographical references and index.
    ISBN-13: 978-0-941936-96-5 (pbk. : alk, paper)
    ISBN-10: 0-941936-96-1 (pbk. : alk, paper)
  1. Furniture making. 2. Arts and crafts movement. 3. Greene & Greene. I. Greene
TT194.P43 2006
684.1"04--dc22

                       2005025372

Linden Publishing Inc.
2006 S. Mary
Fresno CA
www.lindenpub.com
800-345-4447

Contents

6   **Dedication**

7   **Acknowledgements**

8   **Introduction**

Greene & Greene: History and Influences

12   Chapter 1. Charles and Henry Greene

14   Chapter 2. Pasadena

18   Chapter 3. Peter and John Hall

24   Chapter 4. A Divine Collaboration: The Greenes and the Halls

31   Chapter 5. The Later Years: The Greenes and the Halls

35   Chapter 6. Gustav Stickley and Greene and Greene

Projects for the Workshop:
Producing Your Own Greene & Greene Details

40   Chapter 7. The Greene and Green Details

43   Chapter 8. Blacker Leg Indent Detail

51   Chapter 9. Blacker Brackets

58   Chapter 10. The Cloud Lift Detail

62   Chapter 11. The Ebony Plugs

70   Chapter 12. The Relief Detail

74   Chapter 13. Breadboard Construction with Exposed Ebony Spline

82   Chapter 14. Pulls and Hardware

91   Chapter 15. Proud Finger Jointed Drawers

98   Chapter 16. Greene and Greene Finishing

Greene & Greene Today:
Interpretations by Modern Craftsmen

101   Chapter 17. Greene and Greene: Striking Out On Your Own!

104   Chapter 18. Arnold d'Epagnier, Furniture Designer

108   Chapter 19. Thomas Stangeland, Artist and Craftsman

112   Chapter 20. Darrell Peart, Furniture Maker

117   Chapter 21. Furniture Drawings

124   **Resources**

126   **Bibliography**

127   **Index**

page 19.

page 55.

page 114.

Dedication

To my wife Terry, whose undying support and
creative counsel I deeply value.

But also to my Mother, who taught me to appreciate art, and
my Father, who taught me the value of honest labor. Art and
honest labor: the essence of the Arts and Crafts Movement.

Acknowledgements

I would like to thank Charles, Henry, Peter and John for the inspiration they have given me. I am truly grateful to the Hall family: Robert Hall, Marilyn Zaiss, and especially Gary Hall, for letting us into their homes and sharing their family history.

I would also like to thank: Bruce Smith for his numerous acts of help and for so freely sharing his wealth of Greene and Greene knowledge and insight; Ted Bosley for his support, and especially for his dedication to preserving the legacy of Greene and Greene; Alan Marks for all his help and for that wonderful article in Fine Woodworking so many years ago; Richard Muller, a true fan of Greene and Greene, for his undying enthusiasm and support; Ted Wells for his help, but most importantly for his ongoing efforts to secure the legacy of Greene and Greene for future generations.

Thanks to Len Lewin for putting me in touch with Richard Sorsky, Richard Sorsky for the opportunity to write the book, Kent Sorsky for his patience and superb editing, and John Kelsey for putting the package together.

Thanks to: Dave Munroe and the Sigma Phi Fraternity, William Benson, Jim Ipekjian, Todd Olson, Mark & Phaedra Ledbetter, Ann Scheid, Wiley Horne, Rudy Michaelis, and Jeff Johnson. I want to express my deep appreciation to everyone at the archives: The Huntington, the Environmental Design Archives at U.C. Berkeley, the Gamble House, Jessica Smith, Ann Mallek, Ann Scheid, and Carrie McDade.

Thanks to Robert Anderson for all his help in the shop and with the book.

Thank you to Julia Mullins (my daughter) and to Jeff Zagun for their photography.

Thank you Don & Gert Sargent (my father- and mother in-law) for the use of your motor home, and thanks Clay Curtiss for your frequent assistance and for playing "remote navigator" while we were traveling in the motor home and he was at work.

And finally, deepest thanks to my wife Terry for all her help and sacrifices, and for a wonderful California summer (in her parents' motor home) researching the book.

Darrell Peart, Renton WA., August 2005

Introduction

People with a strong interest in the American Arts & Crafts Movement are already quite familiar with the work of the brothers Charles and Henry Greene, but it has only been recently that their designs have begun to gain a wider audience. In July of 2003, I showed my own Greene & Greene-inspired furniture at the Bellevue Arts Fair near Seattle. This particular fair tends to attract a knowledgeable art crowd, yet I was still fully prepared to spend my day repeating a short narrative of Greene & Greene and their relationship to the Arts & Crafts Movement. As it turned out, my rehearsed discourse went mostly unheard—few people needed to hear it. The broader world of art, it seems, has assimilated Greene & Greene, and while the general public is mostly unaware of them, they have unknowingly witnessed the impact of Greene & Greene in their daily lives.

The Greenes have had a widespread influence on contemporary architecture: both Disney's new Grand Californian Hotel and the Lodge at Torrey Pines in San Diego are openly Greene & Greene inspired. In my hometown of Renton, Washington, the new central bus terminal sports a steel beam structure which includes details very reminiscent of the wooden beams with metal strapping that the Greenes so successfully incorporated into their famous Ultimate Bungalows. Even tract housing designs now frequently utilize Greene & Greene-inspired detailing. As a furniture maker, I am particularly keen to observe how the Greene & Greene influence affects the furniture industry. For example, it is now common to see "cloud lifts" and "proud pegs" on a variety of furniture designs. In the not too distant future, I hope that the term "Greene & Greene" achieves the stature in the mind of the general furniture-buying public that the brothers so richly deserve.

All of this increased awareness is quite heartening to me. For years I have followed with intense interest all that has been written about Charles and Henry Greene and their collaborators, the Hall brothers. If you're similarly entranced by the work of these master craftsmen you might appreciate the little incident I am about to relate—a situation where my passionate curiosity about all things Greene & Greene got the better of me:

Greene & Greene furniture is exceedingly rare; in fact it was made to order only once, for a specific client. You can't go to your local antique shop and pull out a drawer for a closer look as you would a piece of Stickley furniture. Therefore woodworkers wanting a closer examination of a Greene & Greene piece—a real hands-on look inside—sometimes find themselves resorting to clandestine methods, such as I once did. Some years back there was an exhibit of American Arts & Crafts Furniture at the Tacoma Art Museum. I noticed that the guard's attention was fixated on my nine-year-old daughter Julia, who was getting too near the exhibits for his comfort. Recognizing an opportunity, I sent Julia across the room as a diversion with instructions to look closely at the furniture there, but not to touch it. While the guard was pre-occupied with my daughter, I casually walked to the other side of the room and pulled open the drawer on a Greene & Greene piece, a nightstand as it happened. My principles were compromised, but my curiosity was satisfied.

I know many woodworkers in that situation would be sorely tempted to pull the same stunt! In fact, it's the kinship I feel toward others who are longing to know more that inspired me to write this book. My main goal is to remove that curiosity from the minds of woodworkers by showing them how the drawers are made—what's behind the doors—detailing any place I can peer into in order to better tell the furniture's story.

There have been several wonderful books on the subject of Greene & Greene. I have read them all and my copies

1. *Crest rail of Thorsen House dining room chair.*

are well-worn. There have also been a number of magazine articles over the past 25 years that have partially dealt with the subject of Greene & Greene furniture—but none of them have been completely focused on the specific elements of what we now recognize as the Greene & Greene style. It is the intent of this book to fully demonstrate with photos and step-by-step instructions the details that make up the Greene & Greene approach, for it is this collection of many small details that define the style. Whether Charles found those details in a Japanese motif or from a discussion with John Hall over some construction matter, it was Charles' vision and genius that assembled those details into a divine vocabulary. In this book I present some of them to you for examination, not as a guide for reproducing exact copies of Greene & Greene pieces, but rather as a toolbox to draw upon for new designs.

Of interest to both the woodworker and the historian, I also document construction methods used by the Hall Brothers in their furniture-making to create Greene & Greene furniture. There has been criticism of some American Arts & Crafts furniture for sometimes using faux exposed joinery, and there are Greene & Greene instances of faux "buttons" or spines as seen by x-rays taken by the Los Angeles County Museum. Greene & Greene furniture, however, did not suffer in sound con-

struction because of this, nor do I feel that the usage of these stylistic elements degraded the furniture's' stature in any way.

To better understand what was being done, one must look closer not only at the furniture itself, but also at Charles Greene and the Hall brothers. Unlike the faux joinery of some Arts & Crafts furniture, the Greenes' faux details were not a matter of expediency, but rather of artistic expression. They treated the inside and backs of furniture with the same care as the more visible areas. For instance, the backs were fully detailed (with proud ebony buttons, for example, and fully finished). In comparison, the backs of most other furniture of the era was often unfinished with just shiplap construction.

To Charles Greene, aesthetics was as important as sound construction. A "faux button" placed for the purpose of balancing the design was of equal importance as one whose function was a matter of genuine joinery. In their early years, the Greene brothers received practical training in furniture construction from their time at the Washington Manual School in St Louis, and the Hall brothers were highly skilled traditional Swedish furniture makers who took great pride in their work. Both sets of brothers and the craftsmen that worked with them honored both sound construction and artistic expression—and neither aspect suffered.

2. The back of the Gamble House master bedroom chair.

3. Back of the Gamble House living room rocker.

I explore this and related concepts in depth in the first section of the book, which is devoted to presenting an overview of both the Greene and Hall brothers' history and influences. Coming from the viewpoint of a furniture maker/designer, this presentation may perhaps put the subject in a new light for already-confirmed Greene & Greene fans.

A topic of particular personal fascination worth mentioning here, and which is discussed in this first part of the book is the collaboration between Charles and Henry Greene with the brothers Peter and John Hall, who actually built the furniture that Charles Greene designed. This remarkable partnership flourished during the Greene's famous Ultimate Bungalow period. Charles Greene was clearly a genius at design, yet he knew much more about the practical aspects of woodworking than an architect normally would. Conversely, John Hall was a master craftsman of the highest order, yet he was sensitive to the subtleties of design to a degree far beyond most craftsmen. Charles and John, two absolute masters of the highest order of their respective fields, developed such a profound understanding that it has been said that Charles could rely upon John to produce his designs with verbal instruction only and without the aid of a final drawing.

The Halls' work for Greene & Greene was far more sophisticated than anything previously performed for the brothers, elevating the output of their craft to its highest level. While the Halls do not bear any direct credit for the design of the furniture they built, they may have contributed indirectly. What is certain is that they brought to the partnership a mastery of the craft of furniture making such that Charles was essentially given unlimited freedom to design anything, secure in the knowledge that his ideas would be followed up with highly-competent production.

The Halls, unlike previous furniture makers employed by the Greenes, were very sensitive to the consequences of decisions made at the workbench (the use of grain, for example). I have worked in enough shops to realize that the best design can go awry if left to a builder who is unperceptive and unmotivated. The Halls were not only master technicians, but they also carried out their work with profound sensitivity and integrity.

John Hall reportedly possessed a quiet, artistic temperament. Some of John's surviving non-Greene & Greene work would surely suggest his creative nature. But how

4. *Detail from the Thorsen House dining room table.*

much did John Hall contribute to the mix? Did he, with his impressive woodworking skills and knowledge, suggest joinery that Charles in turn transformed into an integral part of the design? Could the Halls' tradition of Swedish woodworking have been another influence on Charles just as Stickley or Japanese motifs were? Given John's sensitivity to design, could he have made any suggestions concerning design details that Charles found of value?

Any assignment of contribution would at best be only speculation. I feel whatever the contribution the Halls may have made, that Charles was in complete control of the process and it was his vision alone that created the Greene & Green style of furniture. On the other hand, I also truly believe that were it not for the Halls, and the craftsman employed by them, the furniture of Greene & Greene would probably not have risen to the heights that it did.

The bulk of this book is devoted to arming the amateur woodworker with the skills to produce the particular details that make up the Greene & Greene vocabulary. Practical step-by-step instructions will provide you with the know-how to tackle a Greene & Greene project. I have been woodworking long enough to realize that my way is not the only way. This work is presented as a start-

ing point. You may wish to adopt my methods or you may use them as a starting point and then improve upon them.

Finally, in the book's third section, I have highlighted the work of myself and two other contemporary Greene & Greene furniture makers, illustrating how each of us has taken the Greene & Greene vocabulary and used it—in some cases to develop a new and unique branch of the Greene & Greene style. Each profiled furniture maker discusses, in his own words, what draws him to Greene & Greene, and what other influences have played a role in the development of their craft.

It is my hope to see the style of Greene & Greene continue to grow and expand. I would like to encourage furniture designers and makers to assimilate those parts of the Greene & Greene vocabulary that appeal to them, into their own vocabulary. In this way the Greene & Greene style will continue to have a life of its own.

5. *A portrait of Charles Sumner Greene.*
Charles Sumner Green Collection, Environmental Design Archives,
University of California, Berkeley

6. *A portrait of Henry Greene, the younger brother.*
Greene & Greene Archives, The Gamble House,
University of Southern California

Chapter 1
Charles and Henry Greene

Charles Sumner Greene was born October 12th, 1868, and younger brother Henry Mather Greene followed on January 23rd 1870. Both were born in Cincinnati, Ohio, where their father, Thomas Sumner Greene, was a bookkeeper. During the Civil War he fought with the Union Army as a volunteer—rising from the rank of private to captain—and participated in intense combat at both Shiloh (where his older brother was killed) and the siege of Vicksburg. Thomas Greene's wife, Lelia Ariana Greene (Mather), was also a Civil War veteran of sorts. As a teenager, with a pistol hidden under her clothing, she bravely rode through Confederate territory to bring food and supplies to her father, a Union payroll officer, who at times became trapped behind enemy lines.

The Mather and Greene families were both prominent in New England well before the Revolutionary War, with architectural careers being a longstanding tradition amongst the Greenes. Thomas Greene, who always had in mind that his two boys would eventually join forces in the same career, promoted to Charles and Henry from an early age the notion of pursuing careers related to architecture or the building trades. Their mother, however, being less enthusiastic about this direction, encouraged the boys to develop their own individual qualities. **(5)**

The family moved to St. Louis in 1874, but then in 1879 Thomas returned to Cincinnati to enroll in the Pulte Medical College, while Lelia and the two boys moved to West Virginia to live with her parents on their farm. Life on the farm (a familiar and welcome environment to Charles and Henry, who had enjoyed summers there in previous years) served to enhance the boys' appreciation of nature, and in later years they would look back on this time with great fondness. When Thomas Greene graduated from medical college in 1882, he brought his family together again in St Louis, where he opened a successful practice as a homeopathic doctor.

In 1884 Thomas Greene, in keeping with his desire for his sons to embark upon a career in architecture, enrolled Charles, now fifteen, in the three year Manual Training School program at the Polytechnic Institute of Washington University in St. Louis. Henry was enrolled the following year. Calvin Milton Woodward founded the school in 1879 on principles very much in accord with the philosophy of the Arts and Crafts Movement. The school motto was The Cultured Mind—The Skillful Hand; a student's day was divided evenly between intellectual and manual labor, with a premium placed upon creativity. The Manual Training School must have deeply impacted the young Greenes' sensitivity to and fundamental understanding of craftsmanship.

Charles graduated from the Training School in 1887, and the following year his father arranged for him to work as an apprentice (without pay) for an architectural firm in St. Louis. Upon Henry's graduation from the Manual Training School in 1888, both boys were enrolled in the two year Partial Course in the architecture program at the Massachusetts Institute of Technology at Boston. Interestingly, Charles and Henry felt that some of the classes at MIT suppressed the imagination and were inconsistent with what they had learned at the Manual Training School. Additionally, certain early influences took root during their enrollment at MIT. Each day on their way to class Charles and Henry would pass by H.H. Richardson's Trinity Church, with its bold use of masonry and other building material. Also, the boys almost certainly experienced their introduction to Asian art and motifs while students in Boston. The Boston Museum of Fine Arts, which was in close proximity to their rooms, contained the finest and most extensive exhibit of Japanese and Chinese art in America.

Following the completion of their two-year program at MIT, Charles and Henry worked individually as apprentices for a variety of architectural firms, changing employers several times. Many of these firms were direct spin-offs created by former colleagues and students of the architect H.H. Richardson, thus broadening the boys' exposure to Richardson's sphere of influence. In time, Charles' independent and artistic nature began to draw him into other pursuits which put him at odds with both the architectural career his father had planned for him, as well as the apprenticeship positions he was occupying. On the other hand, the more down-to-earth and hardworking Henry found the architectural apprenticeships much to his liking (**6**).

In 1892, a combination of health concerns and a declining medical practice caused Dr. and Mrs. Greene to move to Pasadena, California. Upon settling, the parents encouraged their two boys to join them. Charles and Henry were initially reluctant to consider the move, believing their prospects for work would be much better in Boston. In August of 1893, however, Charles lost his current position, prompting the two boys to make what was intended to be a short-term visit to their parents in Pasadena. On the journey to California they are purported to have made a stop in Chicago to attend the World Columbian Exposition. There they would have been exposed again to the Asian influences which played such an important role in their later work: the Exposition included a replica of a Buddhist temple, replete with incredible exposed joinery and timber construction that must have fascinated the young architects. Once in Pasadena, Charles and Henry found the area surprisingly to their liking, and after a short time they decided to settle there and set up a business together.

7. Charles designed and made this table himself in 1900 as a gift to his wife prior to their marriage.
Courtesy Sotheby's New York

Chapter 2
Pasadena

As young novice architects working to prove themselves, Charles and Henry Greene were eager to take on most any work that came their way, but business was intermittent the first few years as they strove to find their own voice. The majority of their early work was residential and offered little if any clues as to the style they would later become known for.

The brothers were in many ways opposites, yet their strengths and weaknesses complemented each other and they worked well as business partners. This is not to say that one could not function without the other—in later

years they workcd independently—but they were at their best as a team, each relying upon the other.

Charles was the creative one whose heart's desire was to become an artist. Although he adhered to his father's wishes regarding school and occupation, he never gave up on his dreams. To Charles, life was art, so he channeled his artistic skills using architecture and furniture as his medium. Throughout his life he occupied himself with creative pursuits—he loved to paint, and in later life personally produced many woodcarvings. It is said that at times, when checking on progress in Peter Hall's shop, he would even take some tools in hand himself to help out. Charles also had a strong interest in spiritual matters and studied theosophy, Buddhism, and the writings of the Russian mystic G. I. Gurdjieff.

Henry was much more the engineer and possessed a clever mind for things mechanical. In later years, when the brothers were working independently, Charles would often enlist his brother's help when faced with a difficult engineering problem. Henry's abilities were well-respected in the community, and he was one of four architects called upon to draw up Pasadena's first building code in 1911. Although Henry was overshadowed by Charles' sheer creative genius, Henry was probably a more accomplished designer than he is given credit for. His designs tended to be linear and restrained, but nonetheless well thought out. He was the eternal workhorse, overseeing the office staff and essentially running the business on a day-to-day basis. It is likely that he frequently took on more responsibility than Charles, but he apparently never complained as there is no evidence of real discord between the brothers.

His good character was certainly evidenced in 1925 when, while working independently from Charles, Henry designed a house for Thomas Gould Jr. and his wife. The Gould's dream was for a Greene & Greene home with an interior reminiscent of the Greene's work from their earlier Ultimate Bungalow period. However, the Gould's were on a tight budget. Although Henry worked hard to give his clients what they desired within the given restraints, when the final costs were realized the project was over budget. As a testament to Henry's honesty and integrity, he voluntarily reduced his salary to bring the cost back in line with the budget.

Thomas Greene, understood the benefits of a healthy social life, both as a balance to hard work, and as a means to make contact with those who had the means to commission large projects. Charles and Henry adopted their father's philosophy and were active in a variety of social clubs and events. Towards the end of the 1890s, in part due to their social contacts, the Greenes started attracting larger, lucrative projects from wealthier clients, and their work was showing signs of transformation.

With business picking up, Henry married Emeline Dart in 1899. In 1900, Charles designed and made his first piece of furniture: a rather crude table for his future wife, Alice White (**7**). They married in 1901 and in March of that year they began a four-month honeymoon in

8. *This is an early table design for the White sisters (Charles' sisters-in-law).* Courtesy Sotheby's New York

Europe and England. While in the U.K., given their itinerary, it is quite possible they were exposed to various exhibitions and examples of the English Arts and Crafts Movement.

Upon their return to the U.S. they stopped at the Pan-American International Exhibition in Buffalo where Gustav Stickley had a display of his furniture. It is often thought that this trip, which introduced numerous new sights and ideas, served to greatly inspire Charles' development as a designer. After the couple's return to Pasadena, the Greene's work started showing signs of real change.

Several publications, including the *Ladies Home Journal* and, especially, Stickley's *The Craftsman magazine*, were now publishing examples of Arts and Crafts style furniture and interiors, and a number of clippings from these magazines can be found in the Greene brothers' scrapbook. The first pieces of furniture to appear in Greene & Greene homes were furnished directly from Stickley's catalog. In 1902 Charles designed and built "Oakholm," his family home, a structure which through additions and modifications over a number of years became a place to experiment and try out new ideas.

By this time the brothers had settled into their respective roles. Henry was present at the office everyday and dealt with most of the routine business matters such as managing the staff. Charles normally worked from his studio at home where he was free to concentrate on design and let loose his artistic potential.

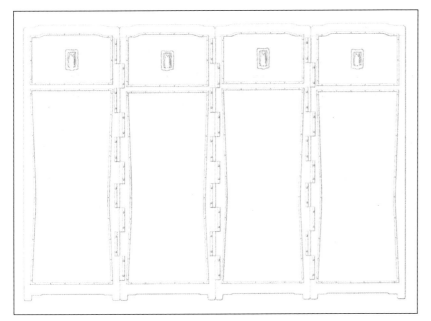

9. *The 1904 Tichenor leather-paneled screen reveals a marked sophistication not found in the Greenes' previous work.*
Charles Sumner Green Collection, Environmental Design Archives,
University of California, Berkeley

In 1903 Charles designed a living room tea table for his sisters-in-law, the White sisters (**8**). This piece appears to be solidly under the spell of Stickley. With the treatment of the tabletop edge this design exhibits just the smallest inkling of an attempt at originality. Given the mature work of the Blacker House, which was only four years ahead, this piece appears crude and almost trite in comparison; the pace at which Charles' designs evolved from this point on is astonishing, and a testament to his genius. Once his creative energies were focused on the work at hand, amazing things happened with great speed and in a big way.

With the 1904 Jennie A. Reeve House the Greenes became more involved with interior furnishings. The bedroom bureau shows a marked improvement in design over the living room tea table of just the previous year. The Reeve bureau, while certainly not a masterpiece, is unquestionably a good, solid design, and still heavily Stickley-influenced. Clearly Charles was pushing at the boundaries but hadn't made a clean break yet. The over-all masculine feel, the through tenons and the white oak, all speak in the language of Stickley. The graduated height of the drawer fronts points to the fact that Charles was becoming sensitive to subtle details. Proud exposed dowel pins are present in this early piece; Stickley exposed his dowels as well, but did not render them proud as Charles did. The pins were quite likely a pre-

cursor to the ebony plugs that the Greene's furniture would become so well known for later. Throughout his career Charles would design his own wooden pulls. The pull on the Reeve's bedroom bureau was probably one of his earliest efforts, but an effective one nonetheless.

Later that same year (1904) Adelaide Tichenor, a friend of Jennie Reeve, commissioned the Greenes to design a large ocean front house in Long Beach California, a project that included several pieces of furniture. Mrs. Tichenor was an intelligent and strong willed woman, she and Charles had what best could be described as a tempestuous relationship. For example, she insisted that Charles break away from his work at hand to attend the St. Louis Louisiana Purchase Exposition (which featured the most comprehensive display of Japanese architecture yet shown in America). In spite of their problems, the Tichenor furniture collection represents an astounding leap forward. Several of the pieces exhibit an already highly-refined sense of furniture design, while utilizing a cohesive vocabulary. The designs are subtle, very well thought out, nicely-proportioned, and quite clever. Charles' work with the Tichenor furniture represents an initial break from Stickley's influence. He was coming forth with fresh new ideas of his own. If Greene & Greene furniture had never progressed beyond this point, they still would deserve to be remembered for these designs alone.

The Tichenor leather-paneled screen is an especially imaginative and sophisticated design; the proportions are pleasing, and the eye has a variety of subtle details to discover (**9**). An analysis of this piece serves as a roadmap to where Charles was headed.There is a slight hint of a cloud lift at the very top and bottom rails of each panel. The sinuous curve on the lower side of each panel plays interestingly against each panel's straight outside shape. The details of this piece are all unified and speak the same language. This piece bears the signs of someone who has fully mastered the art of furniture design (although at this stage in his career, Charles had in reality designed relatively few pieces of furniture). The quali-

10. *The Tichenor chairs present a sound design but the craftsmanship suffered. They were poorly constructed.*
Courtesy Sotheby's New York

11. *The Tichenor desk is a masterpiece in design but choices in grain selection indicate a lack of sensitivity by the craftsman at the bench.* Courtesy Sotheby's New York

ty of design found in the Tichenor House furniture was truly amazing considering the short time that Charles had actually been practicing his craft.

A major impediment to the Greene's goals was the quality of craftsmen they had used up to this point. Charles' capabilities as a designer were rapidly outpacing the abilities of the furniture makers that he and Henry employed. Although the Tichenor project represented a gigantic improvement in design, the craftsmen the Greenes employed were simply not up to the task. The Tichenor chairs were prime examples of how not to construct chairs (**10**). The back legs were deeply dadoed to receive the seat and back rails, with the rails being mitered as they wrapped around the dadoed leg. The dado in this joint removed so much material as to severely weaken the leg.

Along with their lack of technical knowledge, the craftsmen the Greenes employed were not sensitive to the aes-

thetic decisions that must be made at the bench. The Tichenor desk was a well-thought out and clever design, but constructed with a lack of sensitivity (**11**). The grain on the fall front is too loud. It appears to shout above the design and wants to draw the viewer's eye to the grain itself rather than the subtleties of the design. Taking notice of the lower horizontal batten from the lower right door, the grain is again not only too loud again but oddly out of harmony with the other battens. The grain to the far right on this door has the cathedrals pointing down. Tradition dictates that all cathedrals (flames or grain) point upward, which adds visual weight to the bottom of a piece.

Charles needed woodworkers that were not only technically competent but could be relied upon to implement his designs with a high degree of sensitivity. The Hall Brothers were all of this and much more!

12. *A portrait of John Hall, the quieter and more artistic of the Hall brothers.*
Greene & Greene Archives, The Gamble House,
University of Southern California

13. *A portrait of Peter Hall, the more outgoing and entrepreneurial of the Hall brothers.*   Gary Hall

Chapter 3
Peter and John Hall

The Hall family came from Stockholm, Sweden. Peter and John's father, John Jonasson was born on August 25, 1838. Their mother, Sissa Larsdotter, was born April 12, 1837. The two married on May 1, 1863, and proceeded to have five children—John Jr. and Peter being born on May 17, 1864, and September 20, 1867, respectively (two of their three siblings sadly died during childhood). The family immigrated to the United States in 1871 and settled initially in Dixon, Illinois, before later moving to Blue Island and then to Rock Falls, Illinois. On becoming a naturalized citizen in 1876, John Jonasson changed the family name to Hall.

It is believed that John Hall, Sr., a cabinetmaker by trade, passed on the tradition of Swedish Sloyd cabinetmaking—discussed in detail in Chapter 4 page 24—to his sons Peter and John. Both John and Peter Hall were to develop into master woodworkers, but just like the Greenes, the Hall brothers were in many ways opposites.

Less is known about John than Peter Hall. John married Jennie Nelson on January 17, 1894, and the couple went on to have two daughters. He was apparently introspective, as well as very creative, and is said to have been interested in design from an early age. Certainly John's creative nature is evident in his personal projects. A pic-

14. *A unique frame designed and made by John Hall circa 1909, illustrating his sensitivity and talent as a designer. The joinery at the bottom of the frame is quite unusual, as shown in the detail view at right.*

15. *This is a close-up image of the lower left corner of the 1909 mirror frame by John Hall. The unusual joint illustrates John's creative talents.*

ture frame signed "J. Hall" and dated 1909 shows that John had absorbed much of Greene & Greene's style and had the ability to execute successful designs on his own (**14**). Although this frame has many Greene & Greene elements, the joint connecting the sides to the bottom rail is quite unusual and very different from anything in the Greene & Greene vocabulary. In yet another picture frame, signed "JH" and dated 1912, John displays great sensitivity in blending Art Nouveau and Greene & Greene elements, further demonstrating his artistic vision (**16**).

John Hall (**12**) was also a master carver. For example, a personal project, a frieze carving he did in 1913 (**17**), has much in common with similar carvings found in the Greenes' Gamble House. Although it has never been established who in the Hall shop was responsible for executing the Gamble House carvings, the 1913 signed carving lends credence to the theory that John himself may have produced them and/ or supervised their construction. Certain elements are shared by both the 1913 carving and the Gamble House carvings, such as birds in flight and the clouds superimposed over the moon. (According to Gary Hall, Peter Hall's grandson, the scene

16. *A picture frame by John Hall circa 1912, blending elements of Art Nouveau (or C.R. Mackintosh) with Greene & Greene: left-rear John Hall senior, right-rear Sissa Larsson Hall, left-front Albert Ludwig Hall, right-front Pernilla Hall.*

17. *A frieze carved and designed by John Hall circa 1913, which has similarities to carvings found in the Gamble House.*

A poem sent by Peter Hall to his son, Donald Hall, dated September 15, 1918.

My Dear Son,

Mr. Frank E. Miller, Master of Mission Inn, sent me this poem which was written by his brother. I consider this very good. I am sure you will like it.

- Dad

The Man at the Carpenter's Bench
He toiled all day at the bench in Joseph's carpenter
    shop,
By the skill of His strong brown arm wrought stakes
    for the full vine's prop:
Fashioned the yoke for the oxen, fitted the calloused
    neck:
Mortised the beam for the house-top's level secluded
    deck:
Carved the tree for the plowshares straight-grained
    curving beak:
Hewed the logs for the cartwheel's clumsy wooded
    shriek:
Mended the presses while the ripened vineyard's
    clusters wait.

He toiled with his hard worn hands through the
    working day's full hours:
He felt the aching arm, the evening's weaken
    powers:
He knew the slack of fatigue at the setting of the
    sun:
He knew the joy of dawn, ere the heat of the day
    had begun.
His was the worker's rhythm of task and toil and
    rest:

He knew the zest of doing each separate thing at its
    best:
His was the fellowship born of the worker's
    common task:
His was the full sweet draught from the laborer's
    honest flask.

He was the Kindred of all the honest toilers of
    earth:
Skilled Fellow of toil, Maker of things of worth:
Lover of weary craftsmen, Friend of the working
    man:
Master of skilled day labor, forget it ye who can:
Brother of earths slave toilers, come to set them free,
By making all labor holy, as God first meant it
    should be.
This is His heartening message, spread it at His
    bequest:
"Come to Me all that labor, and I will give you
    rest."

I would I had worked beside Him as he toiled at the
    carpenter's bench,
I had counted it highest honor to have held His
    hammer and wrench:
But now in the marts of labor and all through the
    channels of trade
In the reeking shops of the sweater and the factories
    where things are made,
And over the men who control the workers and
    their wage,
Now stands the Master Workman, who toils with
    every age:
This is the word that he utters, hear it ye loafers
    that shirk,
"These are my fellow toilers, blessed are they that
    work."

                                        - George A. Miller

18. *A marquetry box made by Peter Hall as a gift to his wife, prior to their marriage. Peter's original drawings for this box still exist, specifying the different woods used.*

in John's carving may represent a desert property that has been in the Hall family for many years.) Although John's 1913 carving has much in common in both style and detail with the work found in the Gamble House, it is in all likelihood a new composition designed by him that drew upon established Greene & Greene elements. It is further evidence of John's artistic abilities and refined sense of design. He truly was an artist in his own right.

Interestingly, the original Greene & Greene drawings often don't accurately represent the finished furniture. Apparently Charles had full trust in John Hall's capabilities and in his deep understanding and sensitivity to the Greene & Greene vocabulary. It has been said that Charles would verbally communicate design details to John, bypassing formal drawing changes. John's technical expertise is certainly evidenced by his surviving personal work, which indicates a strong ability to competently carry out his own designs, let alone Charles Greene's masterful ones.

Peter (**13**) was the more outgoing and adventurous of the two brothers. He loved to hunt and read history and poetry. He was a life-long member of numerous clubs and social organizations, and as a member of the Scottish

Rites became Prelate of the Knights Templar. One of Peter's favorite sayings was "I can walk both sides of the street," meaning that he had no enemies and therefore didn't need to watch who was coming down the road. Peter's entrepreneurial and adventurous spirit took him to Porcupine, Alaska, in the summers of 1898, 1899, 1900, 1902, 1903, and 1904 to mine for gold. In 1899, Peter and his mining partners became embroiled in a lawsuit after another group of miners erected a flume on their claim. Peter and his companions forcibly tore down the offending flume, and the suit was eventually resolved in their favor.

Whereas John was creative, Peter was more mechanically-minded, as is evidenced by the various patent applications he submitted for boxes and hinges. A picture frame (**20**) attributed to Peter suggests that while he may not have been as artistically inclined as his brother John, he nonetheless was a competent designer. As a gift to his future wife, Lida Alice Roberts, Peter made a marquetry box (**18**) with her initials incorporated into the top (the two were married on November 30, 1893).

Peter first moved to Pasadena in 1886 and probably worked as a stair builder. He then spent the years 1889

19. *A rare glimpse into the Hall shop in Pasadena , showing Peter Hall in the background (in motion with hat).* Gary Hall

20. *A frame designed and made by Peter Hall: an original design infused with Greene & Greene elements.*

through 1891 in Seattle and Port Townsend, Washington, again probably working as a stair builder, with John joining him at times. In 1889 the two brothers built the Wiley House in Port Townsend, Washington (**21**). Peter returned to Pasadena in 1892 where he and John were both employed at the Pasadena Manufacturing Company as woodcarvers and mantle and stair builders. Peter gained a reputation as one of the finest stair builders on the West Coast, and in 1902 he went into business for himself as a general contractor. John, however, remained on with the Pasadena Manufacturing Company, eventually rising from the position of cabinetmaker to that of foreman. Later in life, in 1931, Peter ran for the office of city director (city council member) on a recall vote in district three of Pasadena. He won the election and went on to successfully run for a second term.

Peter Hall first worked with the Greenes in the summer of 1904 building the Kate A. White House, and then again in December of that year building the Rev.

21. *The Wiley House in Port Townsend, Washington, built by the young Hall brothers in 1889. The house is still standing with relatively few outside changes.*
Gary Hall

Alexander Moss Merwin House. Neither of these projects demanded the advanced skills that Peter Hall was capable of. Then, in the summer of 1905, Peter Hall worked again with the Greenes on alterations to the David Todd Ford House. Mrs. Ford's cousin, Laurabelle Arms, was married to Henry Morris Robinson, whom Mr. Ford had been a mentor to. David Todd Ford persuaded the Robinsons to purchase the lot next to theirs to build their new house. The Robinsons contracted with the Greenes for the design of their new home, which included all the interior furnishings. Peter Hall, having worked on the David Todd Ford House next door, was called upon to help construct both the Robinson House and its furnishings. The Robinson project demanded advanced skills that Peter Hall and his craftsman were more than capable of providing.

Charles and Henry were impressed with Peter's work, and Peter, in anticipation of future contracts from the Greenes, took out a building permit in 1906 to construct a one-story shop in Pasadena on South Raymond Avenue (**19**). In 1907, John Hall quit his job at the Pasadena Manufacturing Company to join Peter on the first of the large jobs to come in from the Greenes, the Laurabelle A. Robinson House.

After these collaborations, it became clear to Charles and Henry that the Hall brothers were precisely what they needed to fulfill their potential. John and Peter Hall were craftsman of the highest order, trained in the Swedish Sloyd tradition, and they were able to gather together a group of highly-skilled (mostly Swedish) woodworkers who could faithfully execute anything Charles and Henry Greene could dream up.

22. *The Gamble House chiffonier, c.1908, is a Greene & Greene masterpiece. The asymmetrical balance of the bolection inlay and the tansu-like placement of the drawers is reminiscent of Asian motifs. This piece resides in the Gamble House.*

Chapter 4
A Divine Collaboration: The Greenes and the Halls

With the arrival of the Halls, Charles' imagination was no longer held in check. Whatever Charles could imagine the Halls could execute. The Halls had in abundance what the Greenes demanded in order to fulfill their vision: technical knowledge, unsurpassed skill, and sensitivity to design. With John and Peter Hall added to the equation the change was dramatic. Not only did quality take a giant leap forward, but the style we recognize today as Greene & Greene was able to mature almost overnight.

Both the quality and quantity of work coming from Peter Hall's shop is staggering to comprehend. How was it possible that the Halls could produce such a high level of craftsmanship in such substantial volume? How was it that so many craftsmen capable of such a high quality of work were assembled together at one time and in one place?

Just as the arrival of the Halls helped set the stage for the success of Greene & Greene, so did the arrival of the Swedish woodworkers help the Halls. Adverse economic conditions and an unpopular military draft caused many young Swedish men to immigrate to America before and during the time that Greene & Greene were building their Ultimate Bungalows. Sweden has a long tradition of what is known as the Sloyd system (Sloyd means manual or artistic skills). Originally known as Home Sloyd, it was a method of teaching the industrial arts, passed down through families, during the long winter nights in the northern Scandinavian regions. The ultimate purpose was to produce furniture and household items for sale to the general public to augment family incomes. Furniture making and carving were among the chief skills taught. Not only was the value of the skills stressed, but also the importance of artistic qualities and the need for conceptual drawings. With the industrial revolution and the easy availability of cheaply-produced goods that were previously made at home, home Sloyd began to decline.

With the Sloyd system the Scandinavian countries in general, and Sweden in particular, had in place a very strong tradition of highly skilled furniture making that was widespread among the population. In 1868, Otto Solomon built upon the philosophy of Uno Cygnaeus that Sloyd should become a part of the formal public education starting with elementary school grades. Solomon laid out a list of important points in Sloyd education:

- To instill a taste for and an appreciation of work in general.

- To create a respect for hard, honest, physical labor.

- To develop independence and self-reliance.

- To provide training in the habits of order, accuracy, cleanliness and neatness.

- To train the eye to see accurately and to appreciate the sense of beauty in form.

- To develop a sense of touch and to give general dexterity to the hand.

- To inculcate the habits of attention, industry, perseverance and patience.

- To promote the development of the body's physical powers.

- To acquire dexterity in the use of tools.

- To execute precise work and to produce useful products.

Teachers worldwide attended Solomon's school to be instructed in his system of incorporating Sloyd as an integral part of the general education curriculum rather than as a separate program. While Peter and John Hall were too young to have received any formal Sloyd training before immigrating with their parents to the US, it is almost certain that their father trained them in the Home Sloyd method of woodworking. With ties to other

The Ultimate Bungalows

The years between 1907-1911 saw the Greene brothers at their creative peak, having achieved a distinctive and mature style. They were aided in their efforts by superb craftsman such as the Hall Brothers and Emil Lange (a stained-glass artisan). The Greenes were gaining national attention, and attracting wealthy clients who were sensitive to their work and had the means to commission large and expensive projects.

A memorable result of these collaborations were the four Ultimate Bungalows: the Blacker, Gamble, Thorsen, and Pratt houses (with the Ford and Robinson houses sometimes included in this list). The Ultimate Bungalows were large houses (the largest being the Blacker House at 12,000 square feet). Charles and Henry designed almost every feature of each home, including the furniture and many of the smaller details.

These structures would not have happened if it weren't for the rare combination of ultimate talent, ultimate skill and unlimited budget. While Gustav Stickley's Craftsman homes and furniture were generally meant to be within grasp of the middle class, the Ultimate Bungalows were something that only an exclusive few could afford. The American Arts and Crafts Movement at large placed a premium on inclusiveness, and in so doing the craftsmanship bar was held to a lower standard. With the Ultimate Bungalows the craftsmanship bar was raised to a much higher level, and only select craftsmen could measure up.

The Gamble House is now owned by the city of Pasadena and operated by the University of Southern California. It is open for public tours. To fully appreciate the work of Greene & Greene it must be viewed in situ. Nearby, the Virginia Steele Scott Gallery of the Huntington has two full rooms of Greene & Greene furniture, which include most of the Thorsen dining furniture, the Blacker House armchair, and a re-created Robinson House dining room with all the original furniture in place.

Scandinavian immigrants, the Halls had a ready resource of highly-skilled Sloyd trained woodworkers on which to call upon.

It is interesting to note that the Swedish Sloyd system was very much in line with the philosophy of the Arts and Crafts Movement and with Calvin Woodward's Manual Training School in St. Louis, which Charles and Henry Greene had attended. The tradition of Sloyd furniture making can be seen today in the works of the Swedish trained woodworker James Krenov, who embodies both the high level of skill and sensitivity to design as the Halls did.

With the Halls on hand to execute the work, Charles Greene's designs took a giant leap forward. What was once technically impossible was now doable. Nothing was holding Charles back. Whatever his fertile mind could conjure up the Halls could execute with skill and great sensitivity. The progress towards a unified mature style occurred so quickly it was astounding. It is hard to imagine the revolution that must have been passing through Charles Greene's mind at that time!

A drawing of a red oak desk for the Laurabelle A. Robinson House (dated October 13th, 1906) can be placed firmly in the logical line of previous work by its choice of wood and use of through/exposed tenons. But just one week later the drawings for the dining room furniture dated October 20th, 1906, appear, and these represent a clear and sudden advancement in design. Some of the motifs such as the cloud lift are present, and

exposed joinery still plays a primary role, but the designs have taken on an unmistakable maturity and sophistication. The dining room furniture of the Robinson House possesses a refinement of line, proportion, and construction not seen before in Greene & Greene furniture.

The question of what role the Halls played in this transformation can only be guessed at from this point in time, but for the serious follower of Greene & Greene, this is a significant period of transition. It would be fantastic if we could travel back in time to Peter Hall's furniture shop to an instance when Charles Greene walks in the door to check on the progress of the furniture. To listen in on the ensuing conversation between Charles and John Hall would answer one very large mystery. There is really no doubt that Charles Greene was the genius behind the Greene & Greene designs: the mystery is how did the design process work? How much did the Halls and their craftsman contribute to the final designs? Did Charles take elements of the Hall's Swedish traditional woodworking and incorporate them into the Greene & Greene vocabulary? Was there a back and forth dialog in which the craftsmen might present Charles with a better form of construction, and Charles in turn would transforms a structural element into an essential design element? These are questions we will never know the answers to, but it is a safe assumption that Peter and John had a major impact on the work of Greene & Greene.

Within a few months of the Robinson House, Charles

and Henry were working on the Blacker House. The Blacker House was the first of the true Ultimate Bungalows. The Greenes and the Halls were poised to enter what would turn out to be the most intense four years of their lives. Everything was in place for this divine marriage of the Greenes' unbounded creative vision and the Halls' incomparable craftsmanship. Charles, with his desire to be an artist, had truly found his voice in architecture and furniture design. The designs of the Blacker House were mature and fully-realized. All the major design elements were in play and were being employed with the master's touch. As a result, the four Ultimate Bungalows, the William R. Thorsen House, the Robert R. Blacker House, the David B. Gamble House, and the Charles M. Pratt House, all possess commonalities in design, yet each also possesses its own individual identity.

Several furniture designs of the Blacker House, the first of the Ultimate Bungalows, rise to the level of masterpiece. Unique to the Blacker House is the leg indent detail (Chapter 8 page 43), the double brackets (Chapter 9 page 51), and the pull mounted atop three ebony inlaid bars (Chapter 14 page 83). The Blacker House living room armchair, one of the better known Greene & Greene designs, represents a marriage of art and craftsmanship that is rarely achieved (47). It is both a technically difficult piece to build and an artistic triumph. The real complexity of the chair is not apparent to the casual observer. None of the legs are square: the front legs are parallelogram in plan view and the rear legs are trapezoidal in plan view. The crest rail is so deeply sculptured that it takes 12/4 (3 inch thick) material to produce. The arm is simply one of the most innovative and superbly designed arms ever made.

As with many Greene & Greene designs the Blacker armchair is a rare fusion of the masculine and the feminine. Like the eighteenth century's Thomas Chippendale, Charles Greene had become a master of projecting a strong overall masculine sense in his design while allowing individual elements to exhibit a more feminine quality. The arm of the Blacker House armchair, when taken by itself, exudes a feminine quality in its serpentine transformation from the back leg to the front leg. The sinuous curves of the back slats and crest rails are also very feminine. Yet when the design is taken in as a whole, the balance and overall proportioning, along with the exposed joinery, exude an unmistakable masculine quality of strength and stoutness—truly the sign of a master's touch!

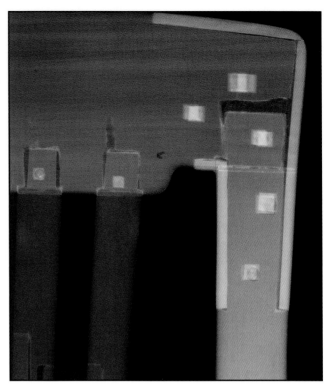

23. *An x-ray of the crest rail and back leg joint of the Blacker House living room armchair.*
Los Angeles County Museum of Art, Gift of Max Palevsky. Photograph ©2005 Museum Associates/LACMA.

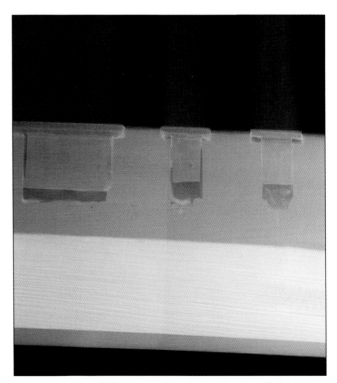

24. *An x-ray of the seat rail to the back splat of the Blacker House living room armchair: note the housed tenons.*
Los Angeles County Museum of Art, Gift of Max Palevsky. Photograph ©2005 Museum Associates/LACMA.

Some critics in the world of woodworking have observed that the exposed joinery found on American Arts and Crafts furniture designs were sometimes "faux." Gustav Stickley, for example, on occasion was said to resort to bogus "through tenons" (that is, his tenons did not actually go all the way through, but instead are falsely represented by a superficially inlaid "tenon end"). Greene & Greene, being a part of the American Arts and Crafts Movement, have also come under this same criticism for the use of "faux joinery." With Greene & Greene the accusation is undeniably true—but the criticism misses the point. The implication is that Greene & Greene furniture is in some way poorly constructed or that to fulfill a desire for expediency the quality of work suffered. This is far from the case. Greene & Greene furniture (with the Halls) was very well-constructed and has stood the test of time. While the Greenes and the Halls were no doubt in favor of efficiency, they nonetheless placed quality and beauty well above expediency (**24**).

25. *A detail of the Thorsen armchair arm: very elegant with an interesting carved detail.*
Darrell Peart

The Blacker House armchair, for example, is replete with faux joinery. The splines for both the joint connecting the crest rail to the back leg and the arm to the front leg are only superficially deep (**23**). Of the many ebony pegs that beautifully line both the crest rail and arm, none have a functional purpose. But yet, as with all the Greene & Greene/Hall brothers collaborations, the chair does not suffer from poor or hasty construction.

Charles saw furniture design as art. The American Arts and Crafts movement and Gustav Stickley had enlisted elements of joinery to become integral parts of the design itself. Charles expanded on this and took it to its ultimate conclusion, transforming the details of traditional woodworking to the realm of beauty and high art, and using them to embellish his designs as he would a purely aesthetic element such as bolection (proud of the surface) inlay. The faux joinery was never a means of expediency. Many pieces of Greene & Greene furniture had countless time-consuming details found in places that would get little or no exposure, such as the insides or backs of cabinets, or the Blacker armchair's trapezoidal and parallelogram legs.

The Gamble House followed the Blacker House in 1908. The furniture of the Gamble master bedroom was especially noteworthy: drawers with proud finger joints and three-tiered carved pulls were exclusively used on several pieces of this bedroom set, and Charles used the pieces as a means to further his exploration of Asian motifs. The chiffonier (**22**) and dresser have an asymmetrical drawer arrangement reminiscent of a tansu chest; the bolection inlay of various woods and precious stones is exquisitely carried out; and the shape of a tsuba (Japanese sword guard) is found in the inlays and cutouts of the master bedroom as well in the shape of the dining room table.

The Thorsen House of 1909–1910, the next Ultimate Bungalow, saw Charles continuing to find original ideas for stunning new masterpieces. It is interesting to note that the Thorsen House was built in Berkeley, California, hundreds of miles from Pasadena. Without the aid of a furnished workshop, Peter Hall's craftsman constructed

26. *A detail from the Pratt House armchair: a sort of cloud lift turned 90 degrees and done in triplets.*
Charles Sumner Green Collection, Environmental Design Archives,
University of California, Berkeley

27. *The Pratt House armchair is a very refined design. Some of its details are borrowed from previous Greene & Greene designs. The arms are similar to those found in the Thorsen House, and the hand hole in the crest rail was also used in the Gamble House.*
Charles Sumner Green Collection, Environmental Design Archives,
University of California, Berkeley

all the furniture for the project in the Thorsen basement, or the "jolly room" as it was called. In any project as complex and detailed as the Thorsen House there are countless small aesthetic decisions to be made on site. The success of the house is further evidence of the incomparable skill and sensitivity of Peter Hall and his craftsman, for the work was executed superbly without Charles or Henry Greene being physically present at each and every step.

A unique feature to the Thorsen House dining room furniture is the lower and somewhat wide rail near the bottom of the legs. The rail has a cloud lift on the topmost edge and long horizontal cutouts in the body of the rail. The cutouts are a very shrewd and elegant mechanism that lightens the rails itself but at the same time lends visual weight and stability to the overall design. The Thorsen side chairs have a very interesting arm that appears to twist (when viewed from a straight-on front elevation), but in reality the twist is a clever illusion (**25**). In side view, the arm is wider at the point where it joins the back leg, but tapers as it makes its way to the front leg, while at the same time gaining width in plan (top) view.

It is the cleverest of devices as it gives the arm lightness

by being narrow at some point in both side and front elevation views, but the arm never weakens because as it becomes narrow in one profile it is gaining width or mass in the other profile.

The last of the Ultimate Bungalows was the Charles Millard Pratt House of Ojai, California. The Pratt furniture was not designed until 1912, five years after Charles Greene had first assembled the Greene & Greene details into a cohesive, well-defined unit. In this, the last of the classic Greene & Greene furniture projects, Charles did not so much introduce new design elements as borrow and refine elements from past projects.

The overall feel of the Pratt furniture is slightly more feminine than past work. The cloud lifts are arranged in multiples (**26**) and executed with a much subtler touch, and at times are so light and delicate as to be barely discernable. The low stretcher rail with cutouts, a device used on the Thorsen furniture to lighten the rail while lending weight to the design, was used again on the Pratt furniture but this time more delicately. This especially

How did they do it?

How was it that so many craftsmen capable of such a high quality of work were assembled together at one time and in one place? Edward S. Cooke, Jr. has done some remarkable research on Greene & Greene furniture and the Hall brothers. In his outstanding 1993 article for American Furniture (published by Chipstone), titled "Scandinavian Modern Furniture in the Arts and Crafts Period: The Collaboration of the Greenes and the Halls," he names many of the woodworkers employed by the Halls. Below is the information from Cooke's list of names in an abbreviated form.

John T. Ball (1867-1943). Born in Michigan and listed as a cabinetmaker for Peter Hall in 1908 and remaining there until 1913 –1914.

Ralph Beal. Listed as an apprentice for Peter Hall in the 1908-1909 directory and as a cabinetmaker starting in 1911 through 1913-1914.

Frank Boynton (1861-?). Born in Maine or Vermont. Listed as cabinetmaker for Peter Hall in 1908. It is believed that Boynton worked on the Gamble House furniture in 1908.

Sven Carlson (1872-1949). A Swede arriving in the U.S. in 1889. Listed as a cabinetmaker for Peter Hall in 1908.

William E. Coolbaugh (1879-?). Born in Massachusetts. Worked for Peter Hall in 1911.

Anton Eriksson. Not listed in city directories but believed to have worked on the Gamble House furniture. He was possibly a carver, which suggests that he may have been involved with the Gamble House carvings.

Frank Holtz. Listed as a cabinetmaker for Peter Hall in 1911.

George F. Jackson. Listed as a cabinetmaker for Peter Hall in 1911.

Horsen G. Kelsey. Listed as a benchman for Peter Hall in 1908 – 1909.

Bror F. G. Krohn (1878- 1963). A Swede who became a US citizen in 1900. It is believed he worked on the Gamble House furniture.

Gottlob Karl Lapple (1877-1948). Born in Wiltonburg, Germany, and relocated to Pasadena in 1908. It is believed he worked on the Gamble House furniture.

John Lundquist (1870 –?). Trained in Sweden and immigrated to the US in 1891. He is listed as a benchman for Peter Hall in 1908 – 1909.

George Nelson (1879 – 1959). Trained in Sweden and arrived in the US in 1896. He was said to be the best chairmaker in the Hall shop. It is believed he worked on the Gamble House Furniture.

Erik Peterson (? – 1970). Trained in Sweden, he is believed to have made some of the furniture for the Gamble House.

David Swanson (1888 – 1969). Trained in Sweden, Germany and Denmark, and came to the US to avoid military service in 1907. He is said to be proudest of his work on the furniture for the Gamble House master bedroom and guest room. It is believed he worked with Fred Krohn on the Gamble House furniture.

Henry Warne (1848- 191?). Born in Ohio and listed as a cabinetmaker for Peter Hall in 1908-1909.

effective on the chairs. The living room armchair borrows its "twist arms" from the Thorsen dining room chairs and its crest rail "hand hole" from the Gamble House chairs. Unique to the Pratt House are the multiple wavy cutout lines found in both the lower stretcher rails and as a silver inlay in the pulls. The inlays of the Pratt House appear to be representative of the live oak trees that grew near Charles' home in Pasadena. While most of the design elements of the Pratt furniture lean towards a more feminine quality the inlays are not only larger but also more stout and masculine than past inlays. The armchair side seat rails taper downward and match the width of the front seat rails, which have a downward graceful curve suggesting the weight of an occupant (27).

28. *The James House in Carmel, California, was designed by Charles. It is a true masterpiece, although it represented a radical departure from his earlier work.* Charles Sumner Green Collection, Environmental Design Archives, University of California, Berkeley

Chapter 5
The Later Years:
The Greenes and the Halls

Charles and Henry

After completing the Pratt House, Charles Greene continued to design furniture, but not in the quantity and never again in the style he had perfected during the Ultimate Bungalow years. The Cordelia A. Culbertson House of 1911-1913 was his only later project in which he designed a sizable amount of furniture, and the pieces, while well-designed and constructed, were more in the Queen Anne style than his own.

In 1916 Charles and his family moved north up the California coast to Carmel. The firm known as Greene & Greene formally ceased to exist in 1922, although Charles continued to enlist Henry for his engineering skills. Henry continued living and working independently in Pasadena where he designed several new homes (and even some furniture) and maintained existing Greene & Greene houses. His furniture designs in this later period tended to be reminiscent of earlier Greene & Greene work.

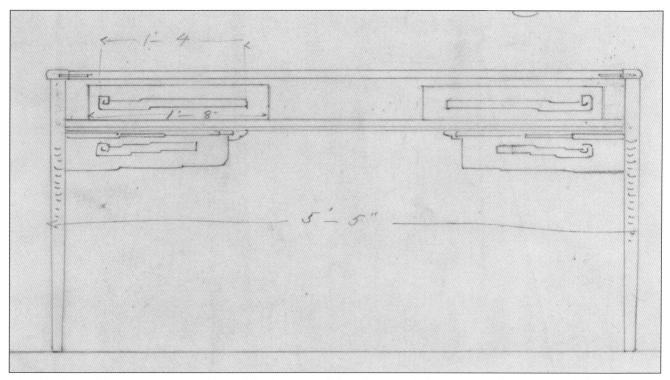

29. *The James House desk was never built. The drawing exhibits elements of classic Greene & Greene work, but for the most part it is a transitional piece.* Charles Sumner Green Collection, Environmental Design Archives, University of California, Berkeley

Charles remained a creative genius. In 1918 he designed and oversaw the construction of the James House—a true masterpiece in stone rising up from the ocean cliff near Carmel, California—which was unlike any other thing Greene & Greene had done (**28**). The surviving drawings for the James House include plans for a desk and dining table that were never built (**29** and **30**). These two designs, and the desk especially, offer an interesting look at the progression from the classic Greene & Greene style to what could be termed Charles' later (and much less prolific) carved period. The desk has several established Greene & Greene details such as cloud-lifts, ebony pegs, and the exposed ebony spline, but the design is lacking some of the masculinity found in previous designs. Surface carving on both the legs and the lower end rail (end view) makes an appearance, a hint at things to come. The dining table with its richly carved detail is essentially not recognizable as a typical Greene & Greene design, having more in common with the furniture that Charles designed for the Fleishhacker game room just a short time later. It is a shame that the James furniture was never built. The rough drawing of the desk offers a tantalizing look at the transitional process going on in Charles' mind.

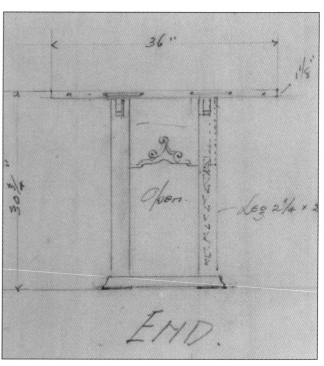

30. *The drawing for the James House dining table (never built) is another transitional piece showing a few links to classic Greene & Greene designs, but having more in common with Charles' carved work from the Fleishhacker game room.*
Charles Sumner Green Collection, Environmental Design Archives, University of California, Berkeley

31. *The Fleishhacker game room furniture, while possessing good solid design, has little in common with furniture from the Ultimate Bungalow period.*

32. *Charles himself did all the carving for the Fleishhacker game room. This is a detail from the frieze near the ceiling.*

33. *It is commonly believed that Charles carved the Fleishhacker chairs, but given the complexity of their construction it is most likely that John Hall was the one who actually built them.*

Much of the furniture Charles designed in his later career was rich with carvings which he did himself. The Mortimer Fleishhacker residence in Woodside, California, or Green Gables as it was called, was the largest of the Greene & Greene commissions. Work began in 1911, after most of the Ultimate Bungalow work was done. The house and design for the grounds were far removed from their earlier work, possessing the persona of a classic English cottage. In 1925, Charles personally carved the furniture and wall panels for the Fleishhacker game room. There is evidence that Charles built some of the Fleishhacker furniture himself—it is very likely he built the game table as it bears his signature and its construction is relatively simple. However the game table chairs are more complex in construction and do not bear his signature. It is believed that Charles did the carving, but John Hall may have built the chairs (**31, 32, 33**).

Peter and John

With the decline of furniture commissions coming from the Greenes, many of the key craftsmen Peter Hall had brought together found employment in other local shops. By 1918 the Halls had concentrated their efforts on the manufacture of small finger jointed redwood boxes for dried fruits and candies. A number of boxes had ingenious catches and hinging mechanisms that were designed and patented by Peter (**34, 35**).

In 1921 Peter Hall's shop burned down and along with it "thousands of boxes in various stages of completion as well as many thousands of feet of seasoned redwood and valuable machinery." (*American Furniture 1993*: "Scandinavian Modern Furniture in the Arts and Crafts Period: The Collaboration of the Greenes and the Halls" by Edward S. Cooke Jr.) Rather than rebuild his shop, Peter focused his efforts on his contracting business, building many homes in the area as well as St. Paul's Cathedral in Los Angles (1923). John Hall continued to work in the Pasadena area, sometimes with his brother and occasionally for the Greenes. Little is known of his later work.

34. *After business with the Greenes slowed down Peter Hall's shop produced candy boxes such as this.*

35. *This is another of the many boxes produced by Peter Hall's shop.*

36. *Gustav Stickley (1858 -1942), the father of the American Arts and Crafts Movement.*

The Furniture of Gustav Stickley,
Linden Publishing 1996
(originally published by Simon & Schuster)

37. *John Ruskin (1819-1900) was an early proponent of Arts and Crafts ideals.*

The Furniture of Gustav Stickley,
Linden Publishing 1996
(originally published by Simon & Schuster)

38. *William Morris (1834-1896) was the driving force behind the English Arts and Crafts Movement.*

The Furniture of Gustav Stickley,
Linden Publishing 1996
(originally published by Simon & Schuster)

Chapter 6
Gustav Stickley and Greene & Greene

Gustav Stickley: The Greene & Greene Starting Point

Every creative enterprise is built on a foundation that was laid down by its predecessors, people who themselves were in turn dependent on the groundwork laid down by those who came before. For example, in the world of pop music, the Beatles shattered all the previous molds and set a new standard, but they did so in part by building upon the foundation that Elvis Presley and others laid down. Elvis was himself, in turn, influenced by the black blues and white country music that had preceded him.

Gustav Stickley's impact was felt far and wide at the time, and he became a major factor in American furniture design (**36**). He was their greatest early influence, and laid down the foundation that Greene & Greene built upon to realize their own vision of what furniture could be. The Greene brothers' scrapbook contained numerous

clipping of Stickley designs, and their earlier commissions were furnished with his furniture.

Gustav Stickley approached furniture design with an original philosophy and viewpoint, and can be considered the father of the American Arts and Crafts Movement. His influence was widespread and his imitators were countless. With the exceptions of Charles Limbert and Greene & Greene, few if any of his American contemporaries improved upon his ideas.

Stickley's childhood was less privileged than that of Charles and Henry Greene. From the age of twelve he worked as a stonemason's apprentice, which was hard and heavy work for a boy. By the eighth grade his father abandoned the family and Stickley had to quit school in order to help provide for his mother and younger siblings. At age sixteen he went to work in his uncle's furniture factory making chairs. He truly enjoyed working with wood

39. *This early design by Gustav Stickley, circa 1900, had a marked Art Nouveau influence.*
Stickley Craftsman Furniture Catalogs, Dover Publishing

40. *This early 1902 Stickley design exhibits his well-known structural style.*
Stickley Craftsman Furniture Catalogs, Dover Publishing

and due to his competence eventually succeeded in becoming foreman. Stickley got plenty of hands-on experience as a furniture maker and it is said that he was a true craftsman—but it was not just practical woodworking experience that was shaping the young man's mind. Stickley was also spending time in his uncle's library reading the works of John Ruskin and William Morris, founding fathers of the English Arts and Crafts Movement (**37** and **38**). Ruskin and Morris espoused a philosophy that was born out of a rejection of the Industrial Revolution and its dehumanizing effects; they believed instead that work should be joyous. Their model was the medieval guilds in which idealized workers found fulfillment in labor that was both rewarding and dignified.

In 1883, Gustav entered into his first business venture, named the Stickley Brothers, with his younger brothers, Charles and Albert, as partners. They designed and produced a line of Shaker-inspired furniture. He eventually left that partnership and formed another partnership which ultimately became the Gustav Stickley Company. With an interest in Art Nouveau and the Arts and Crafts Movement, Stickley visited Europe in 1898. In France he met with leaders of the Art Nouveau Movement, and in

England he met with C.F.A. Voysey and C.R. Ashbee, leaders in the English Arts and Crafts Movement. When he returned home he began experimenting with Art Nouveau-inspired furniture designs (**39**), then settled upon what he called "structural furniture." Structural furniture (**40**) was not only very simple and honest in design, but quite masculine and rather rectilinear, with the only ornamentation being the exposed joinery. Stickley's new furniture soon became a success. In 1901 he began publishing *The Craftsman* magazine in which he promoted the Arts and Crafts philosophy.

Stickley Designs and the English Arts and Crafts Movement

Stickley's furniture differed from that of the English Arts and Crafts Movement in both style and methods of manufacture. The English were not promoting a particular style as such, but rather a philosophy as advocated by Ruskin and Morris. Good design was important, but what direction the design took was not seen as crucial. Simplicity of design was encouraged, but nonetheless many of the English designs were much busier than the very plain Stickley pieces. English Arts and Crafts furniture was mostly hand-made, as true craftsmanship was honored above all else and machine work was discouraged. The furniture was certainly exquisite, but as a consequence of the added labor it was also very expensive and affordable only to wealthy clients.

Stickley's approach was much more pragmatic, as his furniture was truly meant for the masses. He saw the machine not as an adversary, but as a good friend to be called upon when needed. Work that was deemed repetitive and tedious was given over to machines. Work that called for skilled craftsmanship was given to the worker. To Stickley, this was the best of both worlds. The machines did what they did best, leaving the more demanding and rewarding work to be done by human hands.

Stickley's designs were a radical departure from the Victorian furniture of the time, which was poorly-produced and cluttered with superficial ornamentation. A major part of Stickley's equation was that while he wanted his furniture to be affordable to the masses, at the same time he wanted to demonstrate that things of utility, things which are a part of people's everyday lives, should in addition to being well-made and useful, be objects of beauty as well. He transformed the mechanics of furniture making into a design vocabulary—joinery became art. Everything about his furniture spoke of utility and an unpretentious beauty. The fact that the designs were simple and that machines did much of the repetitive work made Stickley's furniture much more common and affordable than its English counterparts.

Stickley also published working drawings of his furniture and encouraged people to build it themselves. These designs were kept simple enough for intermediate-skilled amateur woodworkers to tackle. Obviously, encouraging the public to build his designs themselves was not a good way to boost sales of furniture, but to his credit it is a clear indication that he possessed a genuine belief in the value of the Arts and Crafts philosophy.

Greene & Greene and Stickley: Different Approaches

In the beginning, the furniture of Greene & Greene outwardly had a great deal in common with that of Stickley, but underneath there was a profound and fundamental set of differences in the two approaches. Whereas Stickley targeted a mass market, the Greenes were making one of a kind items. Each time Charles Greene

designed a piece of furniture it was intended for a specific client and most often for a specific placement in the home. Once a design was produced it was never reproduced. The original Stickley furniture was produced in volume and although the price is at a premium today it can be found in countless antique shops all across America. Greene & Greene pieces on the other hand can only to be found in museums or in the homes of the wealthiest of collectors. Stickley furniture was affordable by the American middle class, Greene & Greene furniture was affordable by only a very few.

A particular point of contrast was that Gustav Stickley was in control of the manufacturing process. Guided by the philosophy of the Arts and Crafts Movement, he made conscious decisions as to how and where machines would be used. However, decisions of that nature regarding Greene & Greene furniture were made not by Charles or Henry Greene, but by the Hall brothers. It is quite apparent that the Halls' primary concern was quality and attention to detail; by what means that quality was achieved was not as important as it was to Stickley. However, the Halls were apparently trained in the Swedish Sloyd method, which at its root possessed a philosophy very much akin to the Arts and Crafts movement. The Halls were businessmen and as such were engaged to make a profit, but they were also craftsman of the highest order who took great pride in their work. Their decision as to where and when to use machines revolved primarily around efficiency. There is little doubt that if the Halls had possessed a computer-controlled laser they would not have hesitated to use it for their bolection inlays, but with their stubborn adherence to high craftsmanship, quality would not have taken a back seat no matter what.

All told, the Halls and Stickley probably relied upon machinery to about the same degree, but from a somewhat different viewpoints. A major difference between Stickley and Greene & Greene furniture was the attention paid to the small details. Stickley followed the practice that was common in his day, as it is to this day, of either paying less attention to, or not finishing at all, the lesser seen areas of a piece of furniture. It is exceedingly rare to find a piece of furniture in which the back is finished with as much care and attention as is given the front or more visible areas. Backs are normally placed against a wall and never seen. The back of a Stickley bookcase for example is simple shiplap construction.

41. *A sideboard from Gustav Stickley's 1910 catalog: simple lines, yet a masterpiece of masculine proportion and balance.*

Stickley Craftsman Furniture Catalogs, Dover Publishing

42. *Stickley Dining Table #622 from his 1910 catalog: uncomplicated in design and construction, possessing a quiet utilitarian beauty.*

Stickley Craftsman Furniture Catalogs, Dover Publishing

This is by no means a black mark on Stickley. Some of the finest furniture ever made has unfinished or raw backs. The same mindset can be found in the field of architecture. Commercial buildings, especially from the 19th and early 20th centuries, would have a front façade. Much time and effort would be expended in making the façade attractive, but the building's back and often the sides would, by their very lack of detailing, stand in stark contrast to the front. It is sort of like being swept away by the wonderful dreams at Disneyland, only to peek behind the scenes and have the illusion shattered. With Greene & Greene the illusion is complete and uninterrupted. The backs of Greene & Greene furniture are not only fully finished, but all the care and attention you would find on the front of the piece is accorded to the back, even including the ebony plugs.

The Stickley and Mature Greene & Greene Styles Compared

In comparing Greene & Greene and Stickley furniture, there should be no judgment made as to one being superior to the other—both are worthy of great admiration. Stickley was a man of great principle who energetically spread the gospel of the Arts and Crafts Movement to the American public at large. His designs were intended to reach the widest possible audience, and that they did. If not for him, there would not have been a foundation for Greene & Greene to build upon.

The mature Greene & Greene designs were not hindered by the need to appeal to a mass market. Since their designs were never intended to be repeated they only had to please the client at hand, and these clients were very wealthy and could easily afford the price tag that comes with work that accepts no compromise. With those kinds of clients, and with the Hall brothers at the workbench, the only limit was their imagination.

The Greenes were not content with being merely "very good," and in the end they created something exceedingly rare and beautiful. Their work bordered on the divine. As it matured, Greene & Greene style furniture became more refined and sophisticated than Stickley's, and could well be described as "Gustav Stickley meets Japan." The use of mahogany and the practice of rounding over all corners signaled a move from Stickley's somewhat rustic language of utility to the Greene's vocabulary of cultivation and elegance. Charles transformed Stickley's idea of highlighting joinery to an art form within itself, and many Greene & Greene joinery details are worthy of existing as stand-alone works.

Stickley's designs were for the most part rectilinear, masculine and sometimes a bit massive (**41**). (Harvey Ellis, who designed for Stickley during a short period before his untimely death, introduced designs that were a little more refined and not as overtly masculine.) Stickley furniture was purposely simple and could be constructed by

43. *The base for the Gamble House dining room table is typical of many Greene & Greene designs. It is complex in both construction and design, giving the eye much to explore and appreciate. The top (not seen in this photo) is in the shape of a tsuba.*

the average home woodworker (**42**). Greene & Greene furniture was often very complex in construction (**43**) and many of their designs are unapproachable by many professional furniture makers. As Charles Greene's abilities as a designer improved, he moved away from the bold massiveness of Stickley. He did not sacrifice the masculine qualities of his designs though, but instead, through a sophisticated manipulation of balance and proportion, bestowed upon his designs an equilibrium of both feminine and masculine qualities.

Greene & Greene and Their Place in the Arts and Crafts Movement

Greene & Greene took the American Arts and Crafts Movement to a new level. The movement as Stickley envisioned was to honor craftsmanship and handwork, while being as inclusive as possible. Early American followers of the movement such as Gustav Stickley and Elbert Hubbard strongly encouraged anyone no matter what their skill level to join in. In making the movement so inclusive it also meant that designs were kept simple and the skills required for direct participation were not

raised to a very high standard. Skill and craftsmanship were honored, but it was the effort and participation that was most important.

In England, where the movement started, the original intention may have been to make furniture that was available to a wide audience, but in reality that did not happen. The cost of labor ensured that the English furniture was only available to the more well to do. While the ideals of the Arts and Crafts philosophy were very noble, they were more illusive than achievable. It was a simple matter of economics. As much as the movement disliked the effects of the Industrial Revolution, there was simply no fighting it. Mass-produced goods were much less costly than products whose construction relied upon hand labor, and people with limited means had little choice but to purchase the less expensive items.

The furniture of Greene & Greene was very exclusive without the slightest pretence to make it anything else. Their furniture was never meant to be mass-produced. It was produced once and only once for wealthy clients that could well afford luxury. With the removal of the economic barriers that constrained others in the American Arts and Crafts Movement, and armed with the unsurpassed craftsmanship of the Hall brothers, Charles Greene was able to let loose his incredible creative potential. Their designs were not only groundbreaking masterpieces but often complex and sophisticated.

Greene & Greene were certainly in a class by themselves by virtue of both their designs and the Halls' craftsmanship. It was ultimately Charles Greene's creation of a distinct style blending American Arts and Crafts with Asian influences that set Greene & Greene apart. The furniture they produced represents the apex of the American Arts and Crafts Movement. But in the end the Greenes fell victim to the same difficulty as their English counterparts: economics. The price of labor along with the changing tastes of the times caught up with the Greenes. The bulk of their masterpiece furniture came from just a few short years (after 1911 they produced relatively little furniture), but in that small amount of time they left a legacy that deserves to be admired and emulated for generations. Their designs were nothing less than sublime.

44. *The Thorsen sideboard (c.1909-10) is a Greene & Greene masterpiece. It resides at the Huntington Library in San Marino, California.*   Ognan Borisov/ Interfoto

Chapter 7

The Greene & Greene Details

It has been said of art that there are no new ideas, only new arrangements of old ideas. In other words, supposedly, all individual elements of a design have been done before and originality lies solely in the arrangement and the bringing together of individual elements. While this may be debatable, it is certainly pertinent to what we recognize as the Greene & Greene style of bringing together and arranging details emanating from various sources. Charles Greene borrowed from a variety of origins to produce something of his own that was unique and ground breaking, and in the process he elevated furniture design to the realm of high art. The direction he took reflected the unique mix of his personality, his environment, and the wishes of his clients. A design has its own personality or character, which its creator bestows upon it. A truly talented designer such as Charles Greene instinctively portrays something of him in his creations.

Charles drew upon a variety of sources for his designs. The cloud lift, tsuba, and brackets all speak of the love Charles had for things Asian. He directly imported the cloud lift from Asian furniture designs used for centuries. The brackets that Charles used most effectively on the Blacker House living room furniture are undoubtedly of Japanese influence. Similar details can be found in both Japanese architecture and (sometimes) furniture as well. The tsuba (**45**) is the shape of a Japanese sword guard, with no historical connection to furniture, yet Charles,

45. *This is a typical Japanese tsuba. Charles had a collection of these, and on numerous occasions used their shape as a motif when designing furniture. The tsuba fits between the handle and the blade on a Japanese sword.*

46. *An example of the tsuba shape, as seen in this ebony lined cut-out in a footboard from the Gamble House master bedroom.*

who had a collection of them and was inspired by their shape, used them as an element of his furniture designs (see image **43** on page 39 for a brilliant example from the Gamble House).

Proportion plays a major part of any design. There are endless formulas that profess to hold its secrets, but mastering the mystery of proportioning is ultimately a mixture of experience and innate ability. In proportioning, a designer must consider the relative size of the individual elements, the primary and secondary masses, the negative spaces, and the placement and arrangement of the peripheral elements such as hardware and surface enrichments, including inlays and carvings.

Charles' early designs possessed individual structural components that were on the heavy side, producing designs that were, with a few exceptions, masculine in nature. It may have been that the very masculine architecture of H.H. Richardson influenced Charles. The Greene brothers were repeatedly exposed to Richardson's influence during their time in Boston, both as students at MIT and as young apprentice architects. At the time the Greenes began designing furniture for their clients, Gustav Stickley's furniture (with its massive structures) was much in vogue and quite ubiquitous, and he became a major influence on both Charles and Henry. Thus with Richardson and Stickley as a part of his early environ-

ment, it is not surprising that Charles' initial work also leaned towards large components with a masculine feel. With experience Charles better defined his own voice, and his designs became more sophisticated and his technique more subtle. He became a more accomplished designer and did not need to rely upon brute force to convey a sense of stoutness. He lightened up the designs by reducing the relative size of individual elements, but he also used proportioning to give back the masculine qualities that were diminished by the lighter components.

Balance is a close partner to proportioning and often the two are fused or indistinguishable. For instance, in order to establish the dominant center portion of an eight-legged design such as the Thorsen sideboard (**44**), the side sections must take on a subordinate role. It is the use of proportioning that allows us to assign the center portion its dominant place, and in this case the sense of balance is perceived by the relationship in mass of the two opposing side portions.

Charles brought his own unique sense of equilibrium to the mix. Well beyond the simple problem of relating the primary mass to the secondary mass, Charles possessed a highly developed and rare sense of balance. For example, he would often arrange ebony plugs in an asymmetrical pattern. Remove or move just one plug and the balance falls apart. The same can be said of his bolection inlays, which would appear to randomly sprawl across a door or tabletop yet possess perfect balance. Move the vine or a leaf and the balance does not work. Charles was most likely influenced by the Asian sense of balance, which can often be asymmetrical—but influence can only go so far. The balance we see in Greene & Greene furniture was an innate part of Charles himself. His deepest desire was to be an artist, and this core, intrinsic desire was more than matched by his abilities. In the world of furniture design he was a master artist of the highest order.

As a person with a strong creative drive, Charles was not content with the status quo. His ideas were not static. He was always on the move with new concepts and new ways of looking at old ideas. Often he would tinker with particular design elements or vocabulary from one project to another, or in some cases within a single project itself, and he was constantly introducing new elements to the Greene & Greene style while tweaking existing details. Charles did not have rigid rules guiding his design of furniture: his designs were always fluid, always alive, always in motion—they were a reflection of his unique situation, his personality, his environment, and the events of his life. Charles' character was complex, and his mature designs reflected this fact; many of his best designs were a complex mixture of opposites (e.g. the masculine and the feminine).

The remainder of this book will cover most of the major details that make up Greene & Greene furniture style as we recognize it. For the woodworker, step-by-step instructions will be given for the construction of some of these details. It's been about one hundred years since the Greene & Greene Ultimate Bungalow period and, as Bob Dylan sings, "Things Have Changed." Our world compared to the world of Greene & Greene is a completely different place. The furniture we design and use today often has an entirely new function, functions never dreamed of in Charles' and Henry's day. In the last hundred years a lot of furniture has been designed and built, and many new designs and influences have come and gone. Our lives have changed completely and so have the things in our environment that reflect back and act upon us.

The reader is encouraged to take the following information and do with it what he or she will. Take the design elements created by Charles Greene and apply them to furniture for today's world. If your inclination is to build furniture that feels as though it came directly from the classic Ultimate Bungalow period, that is perfectly valid. If, however, you are inclined to introduce new elements of your own or "tweak" the ones given here, that is not only valid but highly encouraged. Charles borrowed from his environment and followed his own intuition to create the original Greene & Greene style. The reader is encouraged to take that portion of the Greene & Greene vocabulary that speaks to him and create his own Greene & Greene dialect, or perhaps his own entirely new style of furniture—something that is uniquely yours; something that only you could or would create; something that reflects your personality and environment. Your creation then becomes the offspring of Greene & Greene and the style is kept alive and renewed.

On a more practical note, the methods given here to produce these details should also be considered just starting points. Methods of work should not become static, and the author is not the last authority in their manufacture. With the collective effort of those putting the printed instruction from this book to practical application there will undoubtedly arise better ideas and valid short cuts. By all means use them with the author's blessing.

Chapter 8
Blacker Leg Indent Detail

Throughout the history of furniture design there have been numerous treatments for the bottom-most portion of legs. Whatever design device is used, the objective is more often than not to visually emphasize the fact that the legs are supporting the weight of the entire piece of furniture. Frequently this is achieved by tapering the leg as it nears the floor, then the very bottom of the leg will gain mass again, creating a visual anchor to the design as a whole. Most of the classic furniture makers had their own devices for this, and examples can be seen as far back as ancient Egypt. Probably the best-known use of this mechanism is the claw and ball foot, which was used extensively by Thomas Chippendale.

In the Blacker House, Charles was apparently experimenting with two different ways to treat the lower leg. The lower leg detail of the entry hall furniture (**63**, page 49) is quite similar to examples found in antique Chinese furniture. The carving detail used on this furniture appears to be repeated in the overhead beam near the stairway in the entry hall. For the living room furniture though, Charles came up with an original and very clever treatment of the lower leg (**47**). The center portion of the lower leg is indented on a slope creating a fading effect as it rises up the leg. The outside profile of the leg is unaffected by the indent however, but the overall effect is that the weight of the chair is pushing down on, and being

47. *A perfect blend of the masculine and the feminine, the Blacker armchair, 1907-09, is a masterpiece that is quite challenging to build! There are two Blacker armchairs residing in museums: one at the Los Angeles County Museum of Art and the other at the Huntington Library, both in California.*

Los Angeles County Museum of Art, Gift of Max Palevsky.
Photograph ©2005 Museum Associates/LACMA.

supported by, that portion of the leg just below the indent. Although there is no actual overall gain in mass at the point were the leg meets the floor, the illusion is nonetheless there. This is a remarkably ingenious and original approach to a classic aspect of furniture making.

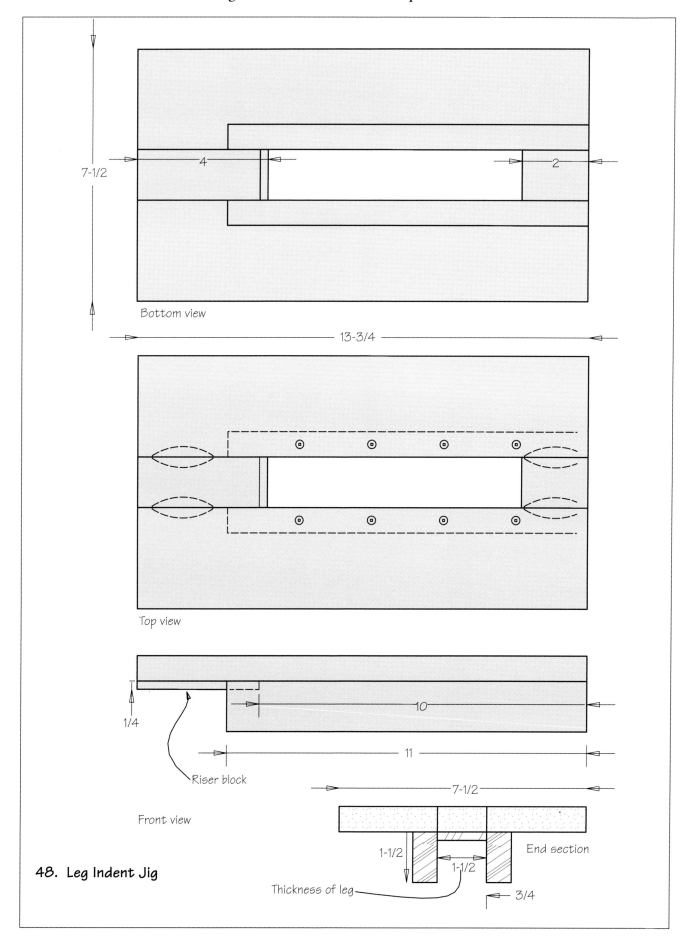

7-1/2

4   2

Bottom view

13-3/4

Top view

1/4

10

Riser block

11

Front view

7-1/2

1-1/2   End section

1-1/2

48. Leg Indent Jig

Thickness of leg

3/4

Constructing the Jig

The Blacker House leg indent detail is deceptively easy to do, at least for today's woodworkers. The Halls did not have the advantage of routers like we have today, and it was in all likelihood a much more time-consuming procedure for their shop.

The first step is to make the jig, which is essentially a routing template with two pieces of wood on either side of the opening to capture and hold the leg (**49**), with a small "riser block" (**50**) at the far end to create a ramp effect. The size of the opening depends on the width of the leg. The jig's platform consists of four pieces—two identical side-pieces and two middle pieces—which determine the size of the opening. The middle platform pieces should be about 1/64 inch wider than the leg being worked on. Referring to drawing **48**, cut out the parts for the jig. Make the platform from 3/4 inch MDF or Baltic birch and assemble it using biscuits or dowels.

49. *An MDF jig and a router with a 1/2 inch bit and 1 inch template guide, representing all that's required to produce the indent detail.*   Julia Mullins

Next, mill two pieces of solid wood 7/8 inch by 1-5/8 inches by 11 inches. Attach one of these pieces, with screws, to the bottom of the platform, aligning it flush with the edge of the center opening and with the front of the jig. With the leg stock held against the attached piece of wood and under the opening, place the other piece of wood against the leg and also attach it to the platform with screws. Ideally the leg should fit so that it easily moves in and out with just light friction between the two pieces of wood. If it is too tight, remove one of the pieces of wood and re-attach it, this time with a piece of paper between the leg and the piece of wood. To finish the jig attach a 1/4 inch thick block between the two pieces of wood starting 10 inches back from the front of the jig. The purpose of the block is to form a ramp (incline), allowing the router to machine an indented detail that fades out to nothing. The jig is now finished and ready for use.

50. *The riser block on the underside of the jig creates an incline, and fades out the indent detail as it moves up the leg.*   Julia Mullins

51. *The stock is placed between the two pieces of wood and rests on the riser block.* Julia Mullins

52. *The leg-bottom is lined up with the front of the jig.* Julia Mullins

53. *The jig and stock are placed in the vice; then the detail is routed.* Julia Mullins

Routing the Indent Detail

To proceed, first set a router up with a 1 inch template guide and a 1/2 inch straight fluted router bit. Using scrap stock for the setup, the leg stock is placed between the two pieces of wood on the underside of the jig and against the 1/4 inch riser block, also at the underside of the jig (**51**). The bottom of the leg is referenced to the front of the jig (**52**). The jig is then clamped into a wood vice for routing. Set the depth of the router so that the bit does not make contact with the stock at the high end of the ramp.

Make a test cut, starting the router at the high end of the ramp and moving it back and forth until the entire face of the indent is routed away (**53**). Always turn the router off and remove it from the jig at the high point of the ramp where the cut was first started. The depth of the cut at the bottom of the detail should be a heavy 1/16 inch (**54**). Adjust the depth of cut accordingly

54. *The depth of cut at the deepest end of the detail should be a heavy 1/16th of an inch.* Julia Mullins

and continue test cutting until the proper depth is achieved. The routed detail should fade as the indent moves up the leg, dying out completely before it ends. Make certain that the indent detail fades completely before it runs into space

that may later be occupied by lower stretchers or rails. With the depth correctly set, rout the indent detail in all four sides of the leg.

55. *Using the knuckle template, mark the bottom of the leg.*
Julia Mullins

56. *Sand all four corner at the bottom of the leg to shape the knuckle.*
Julia Mullins

57. *With a sanding block, feather in any unevenness left by the edge sander.*
Julia Mullins

58. *With a small, cork-lined sanding block, sand the face of the indent.*
Julia Mullins

59. *Ease the edges of the indent detail with folded sandpaper. The edge should be smooth to the touch.*

60. *At the bottom of the leg, near the knuckle, use a sanding block to shape all four corners of the 1/8 inch round-over.*
Julia Mullins

The Knuckle

At the very bottom of the leg is a small rounding detail that helps give a sort of "knuckle" effect. To start, make the template from drawing **61**. With a sharp pencil, transfer the profile from the template to the bottom of the leg (**55**). Sand to the pencil line on all four corners with the edge sander (**56**). At the last of the four corners the pencil line will have been erased from the sanding of the first corner. Eyeball the last corner using the adjoining corner's profile as a gauge. With 120-grit sandpaper and a sanding block, feather in any unevenness left by the edge sander (**57**).

To sand the face of the indent it is best to use a very small cork-lined

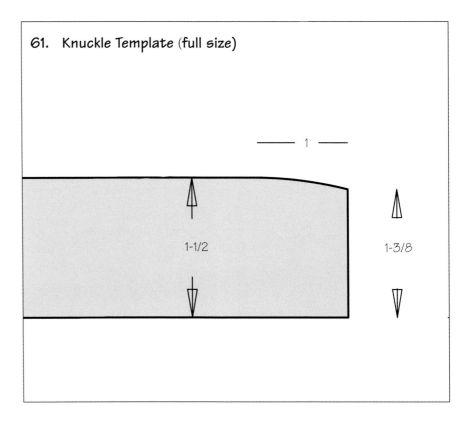

61. Knuckle Template (full size)

1

1-1/2

1-3/8

sanding block about 1 inch wide and 2-1/2 inches long, which can easily be shop-made. Again sand through the grits starting at 120 and working up to 220 (**58**). When finished, the indent should decrease as it moves up the leg and fade completely out. There should not be any noticeable point of transition. The defining edge of the indent is eased by hand with folded sandpaper working up the grits from 120 to 220 (**59**). A good test is to feel the edge: it should be somewhat soft and smooth and not sharp. Rout all four corners of the leg with a 1/8-inch round over bit. At the very bottom of the "knuckle," the round over will need to be created by hand, with 120-grit sandpaper (**60**).

The indent detail as described here (**62**) is not exactly as would have been produced in the Hall brothers' shop, but it is close. If the detail as described is to the reader's liking then use it as such, but if a variation is desired then simply use this method as a starting point. The rate of fade-out of the indent can be controlled by the thickness of the (1/4 inch) block between the two pieces of wood on the underside of the jig. By using differently-sized template guides the width of the indent face can be varied.

62. *The finished leg indent: all the corners and edges are eased or rounded, and the indent fades smoothly back into the leg.*   Julia Mullins

63. *Blacker House entry hall cabinet (c.1907-09) is another classic Greene & Greene design. Notice the leg indents, the carved cloud lift in the doors. This piece resides in the Los Angeles County Museum of Art in Los Angeles.*

64. *The 1902 James A. Culbertson House in Pasadena possesses the first known Greene & Greene use of the bracket detail. The double-looped brackets are located in the upper corner of the window.*

Charles Sumner Green Collection, Environmental Design Archives, University of California, Berkeley

65. *The single-looped brackets seen above the fireplace are from the James A. Culbertson House.*

Charles Sumner Green Collection, Environmental Design Archives, University of California, Berkeley

66. *This single-loop bracket is from the Mrs. L.A. Robinson House, Pasadena, circa 1906. Notice the slightly scooped out shape. In image **10,** page 17, the single-looped bracket used on the Tichenor chairs (circa 1905) is much plumper.*

Chapter 9
Blacker Brackets

The bracket detail was presumably an Asian influence inspired by the low swooping rafters found in Japanese temple construction. Looking back to the 1902 James Culbertson House, two variations of the bracket detail are found. Within the wooden trim work on the wall above the fireplace is a single loop bracket (**65**); and in the upper corners of the window wrap in the dining room there are double-loop brackets (**64**). A single loop version of the brackets was first used on chairs for the Adelaide Tichenor House in 1904 (see image **10** on page 17), and then again in 1907 for the Robinson House dining room (**66**)—but it was with the living room furniture of the 1908 Blacker House that the brackets reach their full maturity (**47**, page 43).

While the actual amount of support given by the brackets is debatable, the double looped Blacker brackets are especially good at conveying at least the appearance of structural importance. The inner (larger) loop gives direct visual support to the leg itself, while the (smaller) outer loop in turn serves to shore up it's inner counterpart. The overall feel is one of stoutness and strength. Charles may have considered the brackets as a form of cloud lift, as the brackets do resemble cloud lifts to some degree (and Charles never used brackets and cloud lifts in the same design). The brackets were never used on furniture after the Blacker House.

An x-ray (**67**) of a bracket from the Blacker House living room armchair reveals the construction method the Halls used. The brackets are quite simple to make but could be a real challenge without the knowledge contained in the x-ray. Each bracket has two joints: one in the horizontal plane and one in the vertical plane. Only one joint in a single plane can be lined up at a time, restricting the bracket from being set in place. The Halls' solution was incredibly simple and straightforward: dowel the bracket in the horizontal plane only, which allows the bracket to be put in place without the complications from a competing vertical joint to contend with. The vertical joinery is then accomplished with a screw running in a predrilled hole.

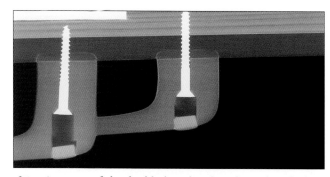

67. *An x-ray of the double-loop brackets from the Blacker House living room armchair reveals that screws were used for attachment.*

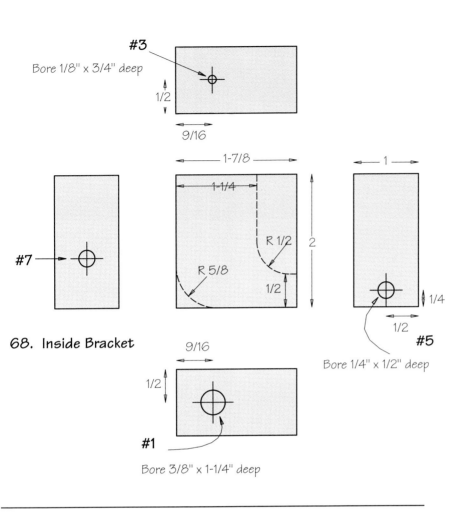

#3
Bore 1/8" x 3/4" deep

1/2

9/16

#7

1-7/8

1-1/4

R 1/2

R 5/8

2

1/2

1

1/4

1/2

#5

Bore 1/4" x 1/2" deep

68. Inside Bracket

9/16

1/2

#1

Bore 3/8" x 1-1/4" deep

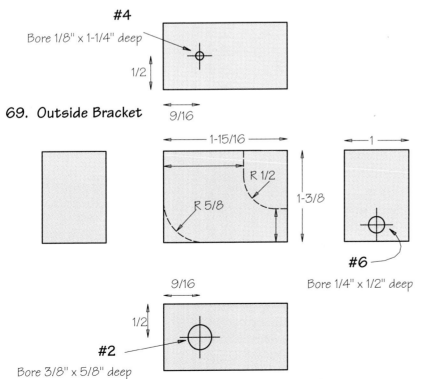

#4
Bore 1/8" x 1-1/4" deep

1/2

69. Outside Bracket

9/16

1-15/16

R 1/2

R 5/8

1-3/8

1

#6

Bore 1/4" x 1/2" deep

9/16

1/2

#2

Bore 3/8" x 5/8" deep

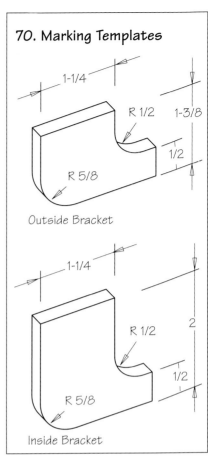

70. Marking Templates

1-1/4

R 1/2

1-3/8

R 5/8

1/2

Outside Bracket

1-1/4

R 1/2

2

R 5/8

1/2

Inside Bracket

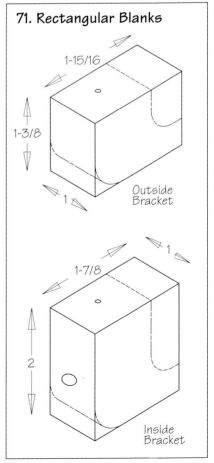

71. Rectangular Blanks

1-15/16

1-3/8

1

Outside
Bracket

1-7/8

1

2

Inside
Bracket

Laying Out the Brackets

On 1/4 inch material, fabricate the two templates (**72**) representing the inside and outside brackets as shown in drawing **70**. A spindle sander is very helpful in maintaining the inside (1/2 inch) radius. Next, blank out the two rectangular blocks that correspond to the inside and outside brackets (drawing **71**). The inside bracket will be 1-7/8 inches x 2 inches x 1 inch, with the 1-7/8 inches dimension going with the grain. The outside bracket will be 1-3/8 inches x 1-15/16 inches x 1 inch with the 1-15/16 inches dimension going with the grain. The 1 inch dimension is variable. This dimension should be adjusted to reflect the same thickness of whatever rail the brackets will be attached to. With a pencil, trace the pattern from the two templates (**73**) onto their corresponding blocks. Pair the brackets up into sets and mark them as seen in photo **75**. Refer to drawing **68** to layout the boring for holes numbered 1 through 6 (**74**).

72. *Both the inside and outside bracket templates are placed on their respective blocks, with arrows indicating grain direction.*

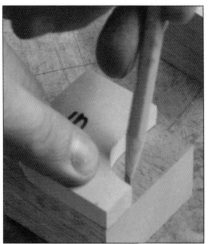

73. *With a sharp pencil, trace the template's outline onto the individual blocks.*

74. *Lay out the boring for holes 1-6 (see drawing* **68***).*

75. *Group the individual brackets into pairs; assign a number to each pair.*

Boring for the Dowels

The 3/8 inch holes numbered 1 and 2 are for countersinking the screw that will attach the brackets to the rail—bore them first and follow up with the screw pilot holes, numbered 3 and 4, coming from the opposite end. The 1/4 inch holes are for the dowels that connect the inside loop to the leg, and then the outside loop to the inside loop. Bore the 1/4-inch holes numbered 5 and 6 in what will be the pointed end of each loop. These holes represent only one-half of their respective joints. With a 1/4 inch dowel point (76) in hole number 6 of the outside loop, line up the two loops in their respective positions against a straight edge such as a table saw

76. *Place a 1/4 inch dowel point in hole number 6. With the two individual loops positioned against the edge of a jointed board, run them together to locate hole number 7.*

fence or jointed board. Push them together to locate the position of hole number 7 for the inside loop. Then bore hole number 7. The final hole (not seen in the drawing), the

one in the leg that corresponds to hole number five on the inside loop, will be marked and drilled later.

77. *Following the pencil lines, carefully cut the brackets out on the band saw.*

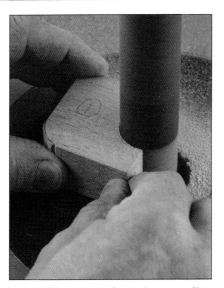

78. *Using a 1 inch sanding spindle, clean up the rough lines left by the band saw.*

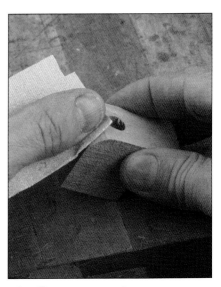

79. *Even out any minor irregularities by hand with 120-grit sandpaper.*

Shaping the Individual Loops

Next, cut the loops out on the band saw following the pencil lines that were laid out earlier (77). Be sure to cut just to the outside of the line, leaving a small amount of material

to clean up later. On the backside of the inside loop, at the point where the two brackets meet, it is critical to maintain the correct position of the tangent point. If the tangent point drifts upward when cutting out or sanding, the joint between the two brackets will be compro-

mised and result in a gap.

Clean up the 1/2 inch radius on the inside of each loop with a spindle sander using a 1 inch diameter spindle (78). With a little practice, the straight line leading into the inside 1/2 inch radius can also be cleaned up with the spindle sander.

The trick is to keep the part moving quickly and to not let it dig in at any one spot. The outside radius can also be cleaned up on the spindle sander. If any minor irregularities still exist after finishing up with the spindle sander, feather them in by hand with 120-grit sandpaper (**79**). Next, on a table router, radius the edges of both loops with a 1/8 inch round-over bit (**80**). All edges get a round-over with the exception of those that match up to another surface in a different plane (**81**).

At the position where the two loops meet, mark that point on the outside loop where the 1/8 inch round over of the inside loop dies (the tangent point) (**82**). With a pencil draw an angled line about 1/2 inch long back from the marked point to the face of the loop. Sand down to this line with the edge sander (**83**), then feather in by hand for a smooth transition (**84**). Re-establish the 1/8 inch round over with 120-grit sandpaper (**85**).

80. *With the exception of those edges that meet another surface in a different plane, radius all edges with a 1/8 inch round-over bit.*

81. *The individual loops are now bored and machined to shape, and the appropriate edges are radiused.*

82. *Where the two loops join there is a visible gap formed as a result of the 1/8 inch round-over of the inside loop: the outside loop must be feathered in to eliminate this gap. With a pencil, mark a line that feathers back 1/2 inch from the tangent point of the round-over, as seen in drawing.*

83. *Being careful to not remove too much material. Sand just to the line: leaving the pencil mark.*

84. *Feather the line to a smooth transition using a very small sanding block and 120-grit sandpaper.*

85. *Using 120-grit sandpaper, carefully reshape the 1/8 inch edge radius that was lost in the previous sanding.*

86. *With a flat board clamped to the backside of the rail and a dowel point in hole number 5, push the inside loop into the leg to locate the boring position for hole number 8.*

87. *With a 1/4 inch x 7/8 inch dowel joining holes numbered 5 and 8, lightly clamp and glue the inside loop in place. Using a number 8 x 1-1/2 inch woodscrew, secure the inside loop to the rail. The clamp can be removed once the screw is holding the loop firmly in place.*

88. *Repeat the previous process to secure the outside loop in place.*

89. *Fill the visible 3/8 holes with face grain plugs. Work the plugs down with either a fine-tooth handsaw or a chisel, then sand flush.*

90. *The finished bracket detail. A 3/16 inch square ebony plug gives the illusion of pinning the inside loop.*

Attaching the Loops to a Bracket

With a flat board clamped to the backside of the rail and a dowel point in hole number 5, push the inside loop into the leg to locate the boring position for hole number 8 (**86**). Bore hole number 8 to a depth of 1/2 inch with a hand held drill motor. Be cautious to maintain a 90-degree angle to the leg when drilling hole number 8.

With a 1/4 inch x 7/8 inch dowel joining holes numbered 5 and 8, lightly clamp and glue the inside loop in place. Using a number 8 x 1-1/2 inches woodscrew, secure the inside loop to the rail (**87**). Remove the clamp and dry-fit the outside loop in place to confirm that there are no visible gaps between the two loops. As before, with a 1/4 inch x 7/8 inch dowel joining holes numbered 6 and 7, lightly glue and clamp the outside loop in place and attach with a 8 x 1-1/2 inch screw (**88**). Remove the clamp and fill the two visible 3/8-inch holes with face-grain plugs (**89**). Work the plugs down with either a fine tooth handsaw or a chisel, then sand flush (**90**).

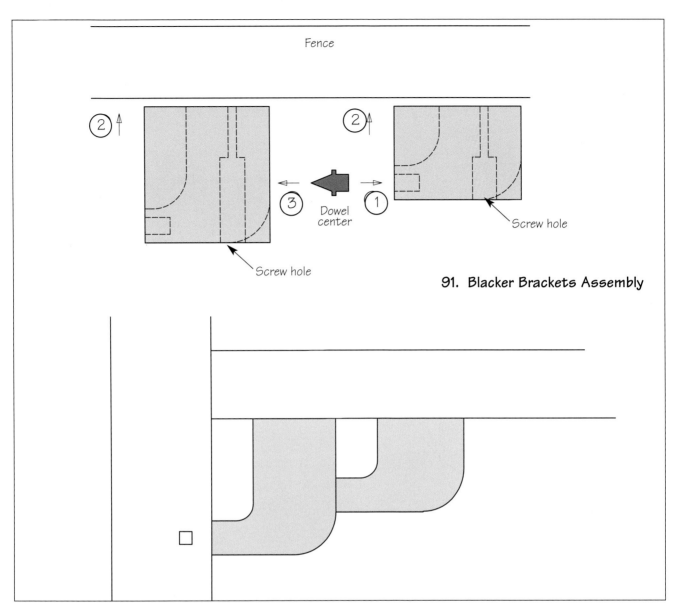

Fence

Dowel center

Screw hole

Screw hole

91. Blacker Brackets Assembly

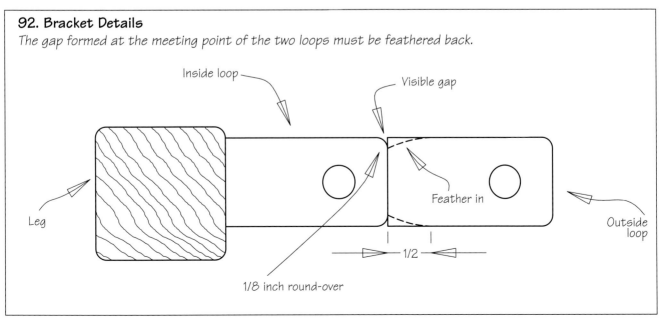

92. Bracket Details
The gap formed at the meeting point of the two loops must be feathered back.

Inside loop

Visible gap

Feather in

Leg

Outside loop

1/8 inch round-over

1/2

93. *Cloud lifts are a rise in the horizontal line connected by two small radiuses. This example is from a built-in cabinet in the Thorsen House dining room.*

Chapter 10
The Cloud Lift Detail

Along with the ebony plugs, the cloud lift detail is one of the two design elements most often associated with Greene & Greene furniture. Originally an Asian motif, the cloud lift—the rise in a horizontal line—can be found on Asian designs going back several centuries. The door panels for the living room cabinet of the Blacker House (see **62**, page 48) feature a carved scene with clouds that are represented as "a rise in the horizontal line." These carved lines represent a direct link to the original Asian cloud lifts and are the very shape Charles employed as a (furniture) design element (**93**).

In some of their early furniture designs, the cloud lift was one of the few things that distinguished Greene & Greene from the likes of Gustav Stickley and Charles Limbert. While the cloud lift was by no means confined to Greene & Greene furniture, it was the Greenes who completely embraced it and saturated their mature work with it. The cloud lift is supremely simple, yet Charles gave it new life in countless variations. He fully integrated it into his design language, making it an integral part of the Greene & Greene style. Without cloud lifts, Greene & Greene designs would be something quite different from the furniture we admire today (**98**, page 61).

The cloud lift is essentially the rise in two horizontal lines connected by two small radiuses, sometimes with a short straight line linking the radiuses. This may sound simple, but there are an endless variety of ways to configure these few elements (**94**). The cloud lift need not be especially subtle, but it should not shout over the rest of the design. There are no set rules in applying cloud lifts to a design: only good judgment combined with personal preference. If not executed properly, the cloud lift detail, despite its simplicity, can detract from a design rather than enhance it. For example, if the cloud lift's radius is sanded by hand it is easy to lose definition. A spindle sander with a vari-

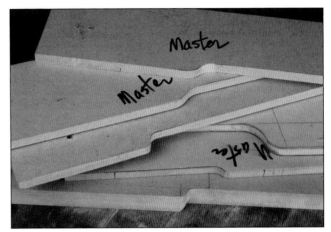

94. *MDF master templates are used to produce cloud lifts in a variety of configurations.*

ety of differently-sized spindles is a great help in maintaining the integrity of the cloud lift's lines.

Making a Master Template

The easiest way to make cloud lifts is to rout them from a template. If, over time, there are many cloud lifts to construct in a variety of different applications, a library of master cloud lift templates may be of help. Each time a new cloud lift size or configuration is needed, a master template can be made on MDF or Baltic birch and then added to the library. That master can then be used to make future templates of similar size and shape.

The first step in making a master template is to layout (in pencil) the cloud lift on the MDF or Baltic birch. Next, on the table saw, carefully cut along the upper horizontal line, stopping the cut just before the blade reaches the penciled cloud lift. Band saw the curved cloud lift lines. With an appropriately-sized spindle in the spindle sander, clean up to the band sawn line (**95**).

Making a Routing Template

Once the master template is made, new 3/4 inch templates for specific uses can be routed to shape from the master template. In many instances, the cloud lifts being routed will only be seen from the face side, such as with a rail or table skirt. In this case screws can be used to simply attach the template to the backside of the stock, and then the cloud lift shape can be machined using a table router set-up (**96**). If the part being routed is narrow and causes the template to be "tippy" a piece of scrap the same thickness as the stock may be attached to the template to ensure stability when routing.

If the part being machined is visible from both sides, a template should be made that secures the stock with hold-downs. Sandpaper is applied to the surface for increased traction (**97**), and De-Sta-Co clamps mounted on elevated blocks are used as hold-downs. If available, a spiral bit is best-suited for the task of routing cloud lifts because it does not tend to blow out as much as a straight-fluted bit will. Even with a spiral bit, caution should be used when approaching the point where the end-grain is exposed. In order to reduce the possibility of end grain blow out, it is best to band saw as close to the line as is possible (without actually touching the line). Several controlled passes at the point of end-grain exposure may also be helpful. If the router bit is dull it may tend to burn on the inside radius of the cloud lift. If this happens, use a spindle sander to clean up burn marks.

95. *When producing a cloud lift template, a spindle sander is very helpful in maintaining the integrity of the cloud lift's shape.*

96. *If a part is not seen on the backside, it can be screwed to the bottom side of a routing template. A spiral cutter will help prevent blow-out. With narrow parts it may become necessary to add support (of the same size thickness) to ensure stability.*

97. *If a part is visible from both sides, a routing template with De-Sta-Co style clamps must be used. The router bit must have a bearing mounted on the top of the cutter.*

98. *The Bush curio cabinet (1908) features a series of cloud lifts in the top and bottom rails of its two doors.*

99. *This is a serving table from the Bolton/Bush House (1906-07). This was most likely the first time the Greenes used square ebony plugs.*   Sotheby's New York

100. *Before the Greenes used square ebony plugs, they employed proud dowels. These are from a curtain rod fixture in the Robinson House.*

Chapter 11
The Ebony Plugs

101. *These ebony plugs are from a Thorsen House dining room armchair. They are in low relief, and sre typical of most Greene & Greene ebony plugs.*

The origin of the ebony plug is somewhat unclear, but the detail can be seen on Chinese furniture from the late 1700's (Ming Dynasty). In early Greene & Greene designs, prior to the use of ebony plugs, Charles experimented with dowels that were both exposed and proud. These exposed dowels, in all probability, came about because Charles and Henry at that time were still under the influence of Gustav Stickley, who had exposed the dowels in some of his designs. Stickley's dowels were flush with the surface, but Greene & Greene dowels were typically proud by 1/4 to 1/2 inch, and the ends were rounded over smooth. They were primarily used to pin tenons, but could have various other functions (**100**), always with a practical purpose as the basic justification for their existence.

Exposed dowels were primarily joinery details serving a secondary duty as a part of the design—their usage was never as prolific, or as artistic, as the later ebony plugs. Whereas the exposed dowels were, in most cases, a very functional part of the joinery, the square ebony plugs were often not. They conveyed the appearance of functional joinery while in reality often serving aesthetic purposes only. The earliest instance of the Greenes' use of square plugs was most likely with the Bolton/Bush furniture of 1906–07 (**99**). From the Blacker House onward the plugs were made of ebony. Of course the plugs at times did serve a practical purpose. For example, they played an essential role in covering up the screws that held breadboard ends on, and in so doing, did double duty as both functional and aesthetic elements.

From language found in an original Greene & Greene contract concerning built-in work (located at The Huntington Library in San Marino, California), the following is typical: "Pins: in all mortise work, and over screw heads, to detail. Ebony squares let in over some screw heads as shown or detailed."

The Greene's perceived joinery elements as art that played an important role in a piece's design, regardless of their actual utility. Charles only placed the ebony plugs in situations where they offered the appearance of a structural purpose. With many of the plugs varying in size and shape, his sometimes asymmetrical arrangements displayed a masterful use of balance. It would be impossible to imagine today the classic Greene & Greene designs without the ebony plugs.

Ebony is the ideal material to use for plugs. Nothing else approaches its warm soft glow, and its deep blackness makes for a dramatic contrast to the reddish-brown of finished mahogany. Because of its extreme hardness, ebony can be tapped into place without fear of damage; and since mahogany is much softer, ebony will define its shape in the mahogany. Gabon ebony, because of its even color, is preferable to Macassar for plugs.

Close examination of plugs from original Greene & Greene work reveals some inconsistencies in the shaping of the face and how much the plug is proud of the surface. Generally speaking, though, the majority of

102. *This is an ebony plug from the backside of a door in a built-in cabinet in the Thorsen House living room. It projects more proudly than is typical for Greene & Greene plugs.*

plugs are in low relief (see images **101** and **102**). A handwritten notation on a Greene & Greene original drawing referring to plugs states: "1/64 inch projection above surface."

Making a single ebony plug is not very time consuming, but just one chair might have anywhere from 12 to 30 or more plugs, and making enough plugs for a dining table and eight chairs means committing to a lot of repetitive and downright boring work. Yes, building in the Greene & Greene style equates to spending a lot of

time making ebony plugs, but the payoff is worth it.

In most cases a hollow chisel mortiser can be used to produce the holes that will house the plugs. It is simply a matter of marking the plug's location and chiseling to a depth of 3/8 inch or so. The hollow chisel will not clean up the corners (at the bottom of the hole) though; it may be necessary to do this either by hand with a chisel, or by plunging the hollow chisel in a little deeper. Alternatively, the plugs can be back-beveled more to accommodate the material left in the corners. This technique will be covered later.

The trick to constructing consistent, tight-fitting plugs is to make the plugs about ten to fifteen thousandths of an inch (a light 1/64 inch) larger than their corresponding holes. A vernier caliper, while not necessary, is certainly helpful in measuring the plugs versus the holes. The majority of Greene & Greene furniture was made from mahogany which, as mentioned earlier, is an ideal wood because of its relative softness and the ebony's hardness. The instructions given here will need to be modified when woods other than ebony and mahogany are chosen. Using either a softer wood for the plug or a harder wood in place of mahogany will require some experimentation to produce reliable results regarding the size of the hole relative to the oversizing of the plug.

Making Plug Holes with a Hollow Chisel Mortiser

Unlike a mortise used for a joint that will never be seen, the hole made for a plug is very visible and must be clean and crisp. The plugs seen on a piece of furniture are a viable part of the design and are likely to come under close scrutiny, so it is very important that the hole for the plugs be well-defined and without irregularities. Be aware that there are certain potential problems associated with using a hollow chisel mortiser. If the bit and (especially) the chisel are not at their absolute sharpest, the chisel may crush and distort the boundaries of the hole. Care must

also be taken to clear away debris that may lodge itself between the cutting edge of the chisel and the surface of the wood. An air nozzle trained on the hollow chisel as it engages the surface of the wood can clear away unwanted debris. If the bit is set too low in relation to the chisel its cutting radius could be larger than the outside edge of the chisel cut, resulting in a "half moon." Sometimes proper adjustment will not solve the "half moon" problem and it may become necessary to file the outside edge of the bit's radius. Finally, most plugs, being a visual part of the joinery, are located near joint (straight) lines, giving an easy visual reference for plugs not in parallel. It is important therefore that the hollow chisel

must be squared to the mortising machine's fence.

There are times when a hollow chisel mortiser is not the most desirable tool to use for making plug holes; for example, the smallest size hollow chisel available is 1/4 inch. If the intended plug is less than 1/4 inch in size there are alternative methods for producing the hole (these also apply if a hollow chisel mortiser is simply not available). The most basic method is to drill and chisel the hole out. Mahogany is somewhat forgiving in that as long as the hole is a tad smaller than the plug, the plug will force its shape upon the hole, even if the hole is slightly misshapen.

103. *A plastic drafting template with graduated-size square holes is available at most well-equipped office supply stores. It can be a valuable aid in laying out the holes for the square ebony plugs.*

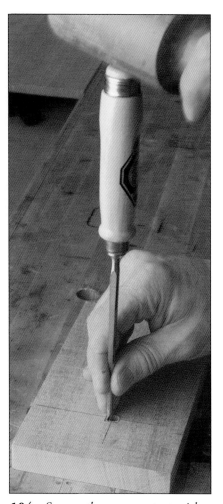

104. *Square the corners: start with a smaller chisel and work up to a larger chisel. A very sharp chisel is a must for clean crisp work.*

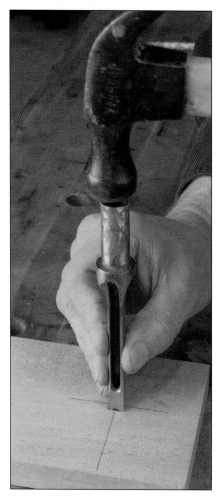

105. *Alternatively, an undersized hole can be drilled and squared up with a chisel from a hollow chisel mortising set.*

Making the Plug Holes by Hand

To accomplish this task, start by laying out the holes with centerlines. An essential aid in this method is a plastic drafting template with graduated-size square holes, available at most office supply stores. Next, locate the appropriate square on the template and line up the centerlines of the template with the centerlines of the layout. Mark out the square with a sharp pencil (**103**). Using a brad point drill bit that is about 1/16 inch smaller than the eventual hole size, drill to a depth of about 3/8 of an inch. With a chisel much smaller than the intended hole size, clean up the corners of the hole, progressing to a larger chisel to establish the boundaries of the hole (**104**). Alternately, if the hole size permits, the chisel from a hollow chisel mortising set can be used manually, in hand with a mallet, to establish the boundaries of the hole (**105**). Then the hole can be cleaned up with a normal chisel.

106. Ebony Plug Jig
(for use with disc sander)

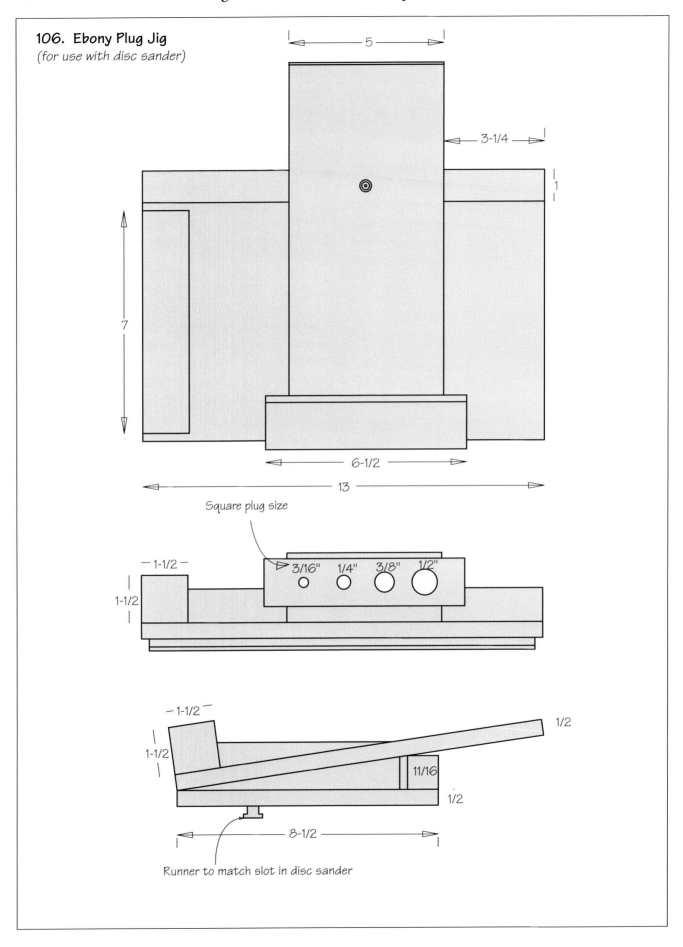

5

3-1/4

1

7

6-1/2

13

Square plug size

1-1/2

1-1/2

3/16"   1/4"   3/8"   1/2"

1-1/2

1-1/2

1/2

11/16

1/2

8-1/2

Runner to match slot in disc sander

107. *This jig can speed up the pillowing process. See drawing number 106 (facing page) for the jig specifications.*

108. *With a little practice a well-defined shoulder can be established. Keep the jig moving back and forth in its slot, and the ebony rod spinning in your hand.*

109. *The face of this plug is pillowed, yet the shoulders are still well-defined. Several plugs will be made from this single rod.*

Square plug size	3/16"	1/4"	3/8"	1/2"
Ebony rod size	13/64"	17/64"	25/64"	33/64"
Jig hole diameter	5/16"	7/16"	5/8"	13/16"

110. *Plug parameters.*

Making the Plugs

Making the plugs is a rather simple matter. The idea is to pillow the face slightly while still maintaining a sharp, well-defined shoulder (**109**). If the shoulder is rounded over or ill-defined in some way, the plug has no place of reference with which to define itself and will therefore lose clarity. Also, the four shoulders must all be in the same plane or they will not seat evenly around the hole. The plug material should first be milled as long narrow stock, somewhat like a dowel rod, only square. With most projects requiring a large number of plugs, it is most efficient to simultaneously work both ends of several rods. If calipers are available, mill the stock to about ten to fifteen thousandths of an inch (1/64 of an inch) larger than the size of the hole. The face end of the stock rod is what will be machined into the finished plug face.

The first step is to form a slight crown to the face of the plug while at the same time maintaining a well-defined shoulder. The easiest way to accomplish this is with a simple jig for the disc sander (see drawing number **106** and **110** and image **109**). Set up the disc sander with 120-grit sandpaper. Fit the stock into its corresponding hole size (see drawing) and, while moving the jig back and forth, twist the stock in the hole (see **108**). With a little practice an even crown can be achieved. It is a good idea to frequently use a sanding belt cleaner as the ebony will load up the 120-grit sand paper rather quickly. (If a disc sander is not available, the crown can be shaped using the method described below, starting with 120-grit sandpaper instead of 150-grit.)

The next step is to smooth out the crown to a uniform shape. This is done starting with 150-grit sandpaper placed on top of a surface that will allow for some give, such as a soft-back sanding sponge (**111**). The idea is to rotate the stock in an even circular motion. When all the scratches from the disc sander are removed and the surface is uniform, perform the same procedure with 220-grit, then 320-grit, and finally with 400-grit sandpaper. The last step is to buff the sanded surface on a bench grinder (**112**) outfitted with a buffing wheel and tripoli brown rouge. Cut the polished plug face along with about 1/4 inch of length off the end of the stock and back bevel all four edges with a sharp chisel (**113**). The plug is now finished and ready to be inserted.

111. *To smooth out the crown and remove the disc sander scratches, place 150-grit sandpaper on top of a spongy surface, and then rotate the stock in a circular motion. Repeat with 220, 320 and 400-grit paper. If a disc sander is not available, you can use this method, starting with 120-grit sandpaper, to form the crown.*

112. *With a buffing wheel mounted on a bench grinder, polish the sanded end with tripoli brown rouge.*

Inserting the Plug

To insert the plug, apply a small amount of glue to the inside walls of the hole. Place the plug in the hole and lightly tap it in with a small plastic-headed mallet (see image **114**). It is perhaps better to err on the side of leaving the plug slightly high rather than giving into the temptation of one last tap to nudge the plug in just a slight bit more (**115**). If the plug is tapped in even the slightest bit too far, its shoulders no longer define its shape, and the eye ends up focusing on the boundaries of the hole itself. If it becomes necessary to remove the plug and replace it, this can be accomplished by drilling out the center and using a chisel to remove the remaining material. If the hole has some slight irregularities, it may be possible to hide these by applying a small amount of glue to the edge of the hole and sanding the surface to produce a putty of sorts that will then fill the small gap when the plug is inserted. If the irregularities are anything but very small the entire hole may need to be slightly enlarged, and a special over-sized plug made for it.

113. *After cutting off the polished end, back bevel the plug with a sharp chisel. The bevel should start near the face of the plug. The rate of bevel will determine the ease of insertion (a little practice will determine the optimum bevel).*

114. *With a small amount of glue in the hole (around the top of the perimeter), and using a plastic-headed mallet, gently tap the plug into place. If too much force is needed to drive the plug home, increase the plug's back bevel. Resist the temptation to give the plug one last tap. Err on the side of leaving the plug high; if the shoulder of the plug passes beyond the perimeter of the hole, definition is lost.*

115. *The finished plug has a pillowed (crowned) face and its shoulders are well defined.*

Seating the Plugs: An Alternate Method

Proud ebony plugs are an essential part of Greene & Greene furniture. They arc relatively simple to produce, yet can easily go awry. Leaving the plugs proud just that right amount can be elusive. As an aid in achieving the correct height try using plastic dado shims. Start by inserting the plug as usual, then lightly tapping the plug until it is securely started. Stack the shims to a thickness (they come in measured thicknesses) between 30 and 40 thousands and place them around the perimeter of the plug. Tap the plug home to its perfect height.

116. *A shim helps seat the plug proud.*

117. *A close-up of the drawer joint from the Gamble House chiffonier is rich in relief detail.*

Chapter 12
The Relief Detail

118. *An early example of Greene & Greene joinery in relief (L.A. Robinson House, 1905-06).*

The idea to place elements of a design in different planes is nothing new. It's been done for centuries, and is found just about everywhere to one degree or another, and in many different styles and applications. Sometimes relief is a conscious effort, and other times ease-of-construction makes it a logical choice. In any event, the use of relief is ubiquitous. Unlike certain other details, relief is typically not such a separate entity that one can point to it and say, "right here is the relief detail, and over there is the breadboard detail."

The relief detail is everywhere on Greene & Greene furniture. Every feature, and every structural element is in relief. Since its use is so common in our everyday lives, not to mention furniture design throughout history, some might argue that relief is not worthy of special discussion in terms of being a uniquely Greene & Greene detail. However, Charles Greene employed the relief detail so thoroughly and with such finesse as to make it an intrinsic part of the Greene & Greene style—it became an essential part of their formula. It's important to note that Gustav Stickley must be given credit for first giving joinery in relief such a prominent role in the design of American Arts and Crafts furniture. It was Stickley's exposed and proud tenons that Charles emulated with the 1904 bedroom bureau for Jennie A. Reeves. Charles further experimented with and refined the relief detail with the 1907 L.A. Robinson House, as is evidenced by the proud butterfly and spline of the built-in seating (**118**). As he did with other borrowed ideas, Charles put his imagination to work and took the relief detail to a new level, making it an ingrained part of his own vocabulary.

The idea of "relief" or "step down" is that adjoining elements reside in their own plane. That is, if you have two structural members meeting at a certain point one is at a different level than the other. Of course Charles did not simply leave it at that. Every corner and edge was rounded over, giving the transition to the next level a softer appearance. The relief detail highlights the structural elements of a design by giving each of those elements a more clearly-defined boundary, and in so doing the balance and proportion between the elements also become more distinct.

The sense of depth created by the change in height of intersecting elements creates not only interesting shadows, but also adds interest for the eye. A good design, at first encounter, draws the eye to the primary focal point, aided by a pleasing mix of balance and proportion; but one hallmark of a really good design is its ability to keep the eye busy discovering new and intriguing points of interest. These secondary details must be subtle in their appeal and not shout to gain attention. As one explores beyond the focal point, the relief detail quietly presents the eye with a series of sensitive details and artful interplay. The tactile quality of the design's surface is also enhanced when in relief. The softly-rounded edges and corners present an enticement for the sense of touch.

Relief, in some ways, simplifies the construction process. Normally a rail and a stile coming together would meet in the same plane and their surfaces would be flush. In order to achieve this, the joinery required must be accu-

119. *The relief detail was used to step down this shelf's underside. It is actually much stronger than its relatively narrow front profile would imply. The breadboard ends at either end of the shelf are in compound relief. It is interesting to note the zigzag pattern of the adjustable shelf pins.*

rate. If the surfaces do not join flush, time must be taken to plane or sand the surfaces into conformance.

In relief, the surfaces do not meet in the same plane and the adjoining surfaces are not flush. The joinery is not as critical in relief. Given this fact, it might appear that relief was the outcome of a desire to expedite the construction process. Not so. While making one portion of the construction process simpler, it has made everything else more complicated. All the proud details such as ebony plugs and splines require individual shaping and polishing. The proud of the surface inlay, or bolection inlay as it is called, requires hours of hand carving

and shaping. Proud finger-jointed drawers (**117**), as found in the Gamble House master bedroom, are not only time-consuming in themselves but unforgiving as well. If a drawer is out-of-square the face cannot be simply planed or sanded into conformity. That would erase the proud fingers in the process. It has to be precisely right the first time.

Several examples from the Thorsen House serve to illustrate the extent to which the relief detail came to permeate virtually every aspect of the Greene & Greene style. In the living room bookcase, for example, the Greenes were faced with the age-old problem of supporting heavy

120. *The relief detail in doubles and triples as seen in the Thorsen House dining room, right below the built-in cabinet.*

books: a shelf thick enough to give adequate support would be quite bulky and clumsy looking. The Greenes' answer was to make the bulk of the shelf as thick as needed for support, but with a series of narrowing steps projecting back from the underside of the front, reducing the shelf's front profile to a visually pleasing thickness. Along with the narrowing steps the shelf has breadboard ends, which are also in relief (**119**). It is interesting to note that this detail normally resides behind the closed doors of the bookcase and is not readily visible. It is a pleasant and unexpected surprise, and further illustrates the incredible attention to detail found in the designs of Greene & Greene (**120** and **121**).

There is no specific formula for implementing the relief detail, but there are some general guidelines that may be of help. When designing with the relief detail in mind, the most basic premise is that all edges get at least a 1/8 inch round over, with the obvious exceptions of drawer fronts and the outside perimeter of doors. When stepping down to the next level of relief, that next step must, at a minimum, clear the round-over of the previous level (drawing **122**). In other words the next level down cannot be in a higher plane than the tangent point of the adjoining higher level's round-over. Neither the radiuses nor the step down necessarily need to be 1/8 of an inch, although the 1/8 inch round-over works as a good default.

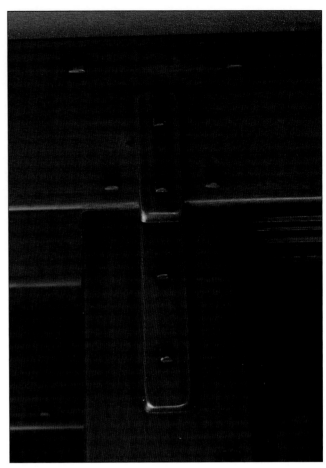

121. *A detail in relief above the built-in bookshelves in the Thorsen House living room.*

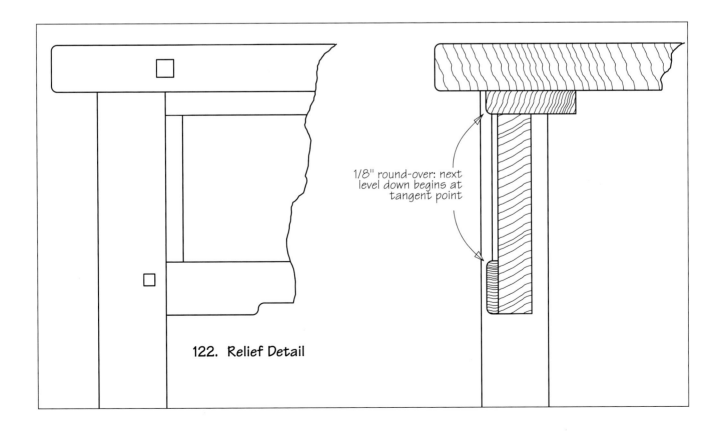

1/8" round-over: next level down begins at tangent point

122. Relief Detail

123. *A close-up of the exposed ebony spline and breadboard detail from the Thorsen sideboard.*

Chapter 13
Breadboard Construction with Exposed Ebony Spline

Gustav Stickley made joinery a vital part of his designs, and in so doing transformed things of utility into objects of beauty. The Greenes took that idea and improved upon it. Charles Greene's ingenious rendering of the time-honored breadboard construction is possibly the highest realization of joinery as art. Greene & Greene breadboards are things of quiet beauty. They catch the eye and are a pleasure to behold, but do not shout for attention. Externally, the Greene & Greene breadboard is merely a series of details in relief, but there is magic in the way light catches and highlights the softly proud and rounded edge of the breadboard end (**123**), and there is a certain grace in the gentle sheen of the proud ebony spline as it mimics the shape which it traverses.

The outward appearance of a Greene & Greene bread-board is to some extent misleading. Although the joint is held together with a spline, it is not the large ebony spline we are led to believe. But nonetheless the Greene's breadboard admirably performs a dual purpose as both an eye-catching design detail and an effective piece of joinery. The breadboard technique is a traditional wood-working solution to the problems of cupping and wood movement. As the name implies, the technique was commonly used on the solid wood breadboards found in kitchen cabinets.

To fully understand the workings of breadboard con-struction, awareness of the expansion and contraction of wood is essential. Imagine the cells of a wooden board as being long, narrow straws that are made out of a dry, absorbent material. When moisture is introduced, the straws (cells) absorb it and expand in girth but very little in length. If the cells were perfectly straight and evenly

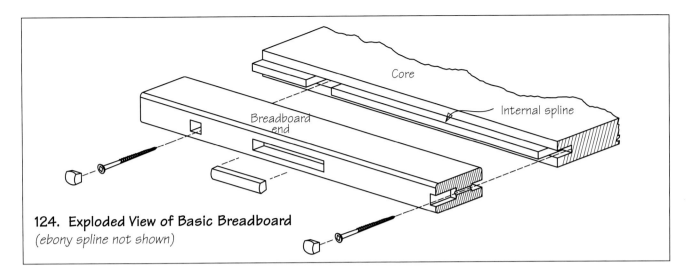

124. Exploded View of Basic Breadboard
(ebony spline not shown)

distributed, and the moisture was absorbed consistently throughout the board, there would be no warping or cupping—but this is seldom the case. The uneven distribution of cells and moisture is what causes cupping across the width of a board. It follows that the wider the board in relation to its thickness the more opportunity for cupping. Breadboard construction seeks to minimize this cupping in wider boards.

Anatomy of the Breadboard

There are two basic parts to breadboards: the core and the ends (drawing **124** and **125**). The core is the main body of the top, with the grain running in the long direction; it tends to cup across its width. The breadboard ends are relatively narrow pieces attached to the core at both ends, with the grain running at 90 degrees to the core. With the ends stronger and less likely to warp in this grain direction, they hold the core in check.

The problem of wood movement creates other considerations in the construction of breadboard ends. The core and breadboard end are joined together by an internal spline. Since the core will expand across the breadboard joint and the end will not, only the center 4 inches of the internal spline are glued into the breadboard end. This locks the core into its position relative to the ends and restricts the core movement to the same amount on either side of the center. Out beyond the center four inches, screws running in a slotted pathway allow for wood movement.

For our purposes here, actual dimensions will not be given for the overall size of the breadboard top. It will be assumed that the instructions included in this chapter will be applied to an already existing project. For that reason only a part's size in relation to other parts will be given.

Laying Out the Breadboard

To start with, make the breadboard end about 1/8 inch thicker than the core, and a heavy 1/8 inch longer at both ends than the core is wide (5/16 inch longer than the core width overall). Keep in mind that since the core is joined to the breadboard end in the cross grain direction, it will be expanding and contracting while the breadboard end stays relatively stable along the joint line.

A note for tops wider than 30 inches or so: there is potential for more movement of the core relative to the breadboard end than in our example given here. To address this, the length of the breadboard end relative to the core should be slightly increased as the width of the top increases. It may be advisable to make the countersink mortises wider (1/2 inch to 3/4 inch), slot out the pilot hole for the screw, and use pan head screws with washers

instead of the flat head screws.

To get started, layout and inspect the parts (core and ends) to determine the top and bottom sides; then mark the bottom sides. Rout a 1/8 inch round-over on all four corners along the core's length. Do not rout that part of the core that will be making contact with the end. On the breadboard end rout a 1/8 inch round-over on all corners and edges, with the exception of the bottom edge which meets up with the core.

125. Breadboard Details

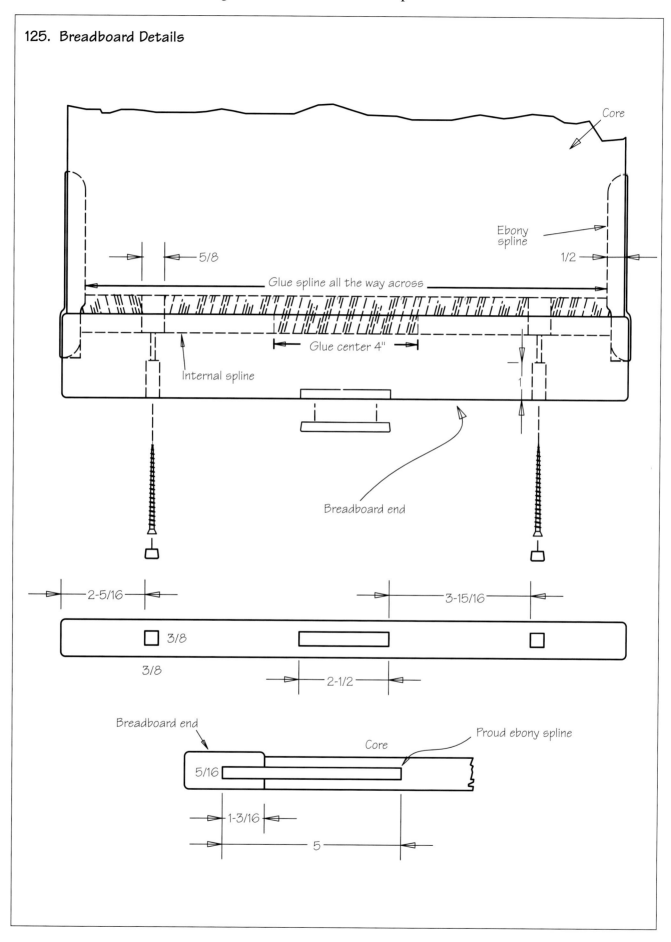

Core

Ebony spline

5/8

1/2

Glue spline all the way across

Glue center 4"

Internal spline

1

Breadboard end

2-5/16

3-15/16

3/8

3/8

2-1/2

Breadboard end

Core

Proud ebony spline

5/16

1-3/16

5

Machining the Breadboard Joint

Set up a router with a 5/16 inch by 1/2 inch deep-slot cutter to rout for the internal spline. Most slotting cutters, or spline cutters as they are often called, do not come in a 5/16 inch width; therefore, it may be necessary to "stack" different size cutters to achieve the 5/16 inch cutting width (**126**). Centering on its thickness and referencing from the bottom, cut a 5/16 inch x 1/2 inch deep slot into the joint ends of the core. Using the same settings, cut a slot into the joint side of the breadboard end, also referencing from the bottom. When finished (**127**), leave the router set up as it is—it will be needed later.

Next, lay out the ebony plugs on the breadboard end. The long narrow plug in the center is for aesthetics only, and its length can vary with the width of the top and with personal taste. The other plugs cover the mortises that serve as countersinks for the screws; they should be placed 3 to 5 inches from the center plug. If additional mortises are needed for a wider top, place them also 3 to 5 inches apart. The mortises should be centered relative to the thickness of the core, just as the grooves were. Mortise in a cavity for the center plug 3/8 inch wide x 3 to 5 inches long x 1/2 inch deep. Mortise for the screw countersinks 3/8 inch x 3/8 inch x 1-1/4 inch deep. With an 1/8 inch bit centered in the countersink-mortise drill a pilot hole the remaining distance to the spline slot (**128** and **129**).

126. *It may not be possible to find a spline cutter in the desired thickness. If so, stack smaller cutters to achieve the desired thickness, in this case 5/16 inch.*

127. *Both the core (or main body) and the breadboard end have a 5/16 (high) x 1/2 (deep) inch slot cut that is referenced from the bottom. All corners that do not die into another corner or surface are given a 1/8 inch round over.*

128. *With an 1/8 inch bit centered in the countersink-mortise, drill a pilot hole the remaining distance to the spline slot.*

129. *The breadboard end showing the 1/8 inch pilot hole centered on the spline slot.*

Attaching the Breadboard Ends

The internal splines can now be milled out to 5/16 inch x 15/16 inch with the grain going the 15/16 inch direction. This way when the spline is in place its grain will be going the same direction as the core.

Since both the internal spline and the exposed ebony spline are the same thickness, it makes sense to mill both at the same time to ensure consistency. Each ebony spline will be about 5/16 inch x 5/8 inch x 5+ inches (the grain will be going in the 5+ inches direction). The ebony spline's exact length will not be precisely determined until the final fitting, so allow for about 1/4 inch extra in length. The splines should fit in their slots just slightly snug but not too tight. With a perceptible resistance, they should be easily pulled out of the slots with two fingers.

Note the positions of the pilot hole in the breadboard end and mark a corresponding location on the core end. Mark a line 3/8 inch on either side of the pilot hole location. Cut the spline material to fit in-between the marked out lines (**130**). Dry fit the breadboard joint with the spline in place. If a good fit is achieved, then pre-sand the core and end to 220-grit. With a small amount of glue in the slot only, and taking care to avoid ooze-out, glue the spline into its respective placement in the core.

Dry fit the end again to make certain that no dried glue ooze-out from the spline is obstructing a tight fit. Spread glue on the center four inches of the spline and clamp the end in place, making sure it is centered on the core and, if necessary,

130. *The internal spline is glued into the main body of the top, leaving a 1 inch space for the screw.*

131. *Only the center 4 inches of the breadboard end are glued to the main body (core). To ensure flatness, clamp straight (jointed) cauls to the glued-up assembly.*

132. *After removing the clamps, run #8 x 2 1/4 inches flat head wood screws in the countersunk mortises to complete the process of securing the ends to the core.*

clamp straight back cauls to the glue up assembly to ensure flatness (**131**). After removing the clamps, run a #8 x 2-1/4 flat head wood screw in the countersunk mortises (**132**) to complete the process of securing the ends to the core. If the top is over 30 inches wide and will be experiencing substantial changes in humidity, it may become prudent to slot both the countersink screw holes (mortises) and the corresponding 1/8 inch pilot hole to allow for extra movement. If this option is exercised, use pan head screws with a washer, thereby allowing the screw

to slide on the shoulder created by the screw pilot hole.

With the top out of the clamps the ebony plugs can now be made (see Chapter 11 page 62 for instructions on making the plugs). The long center plug can be milled to about 1/64 inch oversize by 1/4 inch thick, polished, then back-beveled and tapped into place. The reader may want to skip ahead to Chapter 14 page 82 to read the section on polishing ebony bars.

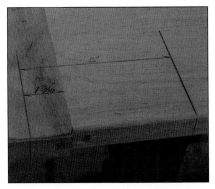

133. *Turn the top backside up, and mark a point on the end 1-3/16 inches back from the breadboard joint. Measure 5 inches forward, then transfer both marks to the edge.*

134. *With a sharp chisel, square out the round corner in the breadboard end that was left by the router.*

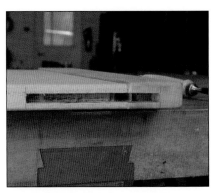

135. *Square out the rounded corner to a depth of at least 1/4 inch. The ebony spline will be glued to the main body, but needs to float in the breadboard end.*

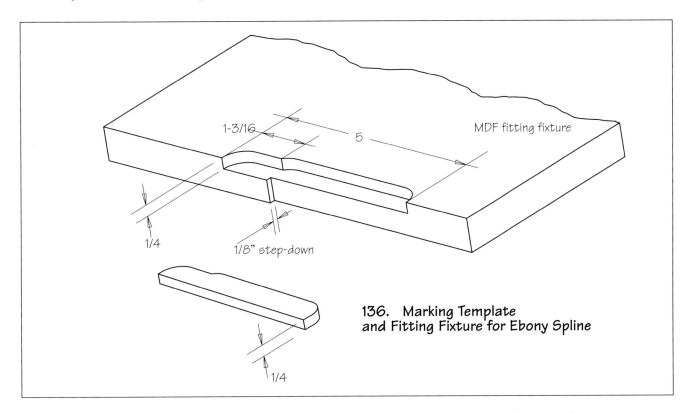

136. Marking Template and Fitting Fixture for Ebony Spline

The Ebony Spline

The exposed ebony spline is fairly simple. Turn the top over on its face, with the backside facing up, and mark a point on the end 1-3/16 inches back from the breadboard joint. From that mark measure 5 inches forward to a place on the core and place another mark. Transfer both of these marks to their respective locations on the edge (**133**). Using the same router and setup that was used for the grooves, and referencing from the bottom, rout between the marks on the edge. There should be no visible trace of the working spline left.

With a chisel, square out the rounded corner left by the router in the breadboard end only (images **134** and **135**, and drawing **136**). The ebony spline will be glued into the core but floating in the end. Squaring out allows the spline to move in or out without any obstruction.

As an aid to fitting the ebony spline, cut out a piece of MDF with a 1/8+ inch step-down along the edge. This step-down mimics the point where the breadboard end connects to the core. The piece of MDF now serves as a fixture (**136**) for fitting the spline. Going through the steps that laid out the slot for the ebony spline, mark the MDF in the same manner.

137. *This MDF fitting fixture mimics the inside shape of the slot for the ebony spline. The wooden template fits the cut-away precisely.*

138. *Trace the shape of the template onto the ebony spline material. Silver or gold colored markers work well on ebony.*

139. *Use the MDF fitting fixture to test the newly cut ebony spline. The cut-away should reveal any adjustments still needed for the ebony spline to perfectly fit.*

140. *With the spline dry fitted into the groove, mark a 1/16 inch line out from the profile of the top. Leave extra room where the core meets the breadboard end.*

Using the same router set-up as was used for the splines, adjust the height of the bit so it will no longer cut a groove but will remove about 1/4 inch of material from the surface. Rout between the layout lines on the MDF. This should now be essentially a cut-away view of the groove for the ebony spline. On a piece of 1/4 inch material produce a marking template that will fit in the routed out area of the MDF (**137**). Using a marker such as a silver Sharpie, lay out the shape of the template onto the ebony spline stock that was cut out earlier (**138**).

After band sawing the ebony spline, test fit it in the MDF fitting fixture (**139**). The fitting fixture should make it a simple matter to see any high spots that are restricting a good fit. After a satisfactory fit has been achieved, place the spline in the actual groove and mark a line that is no less than 1/16 inch out from the edge of the groove (**140**). Remove the ebony and band saw to the marked line, then glue the ebony spline into the core side only.

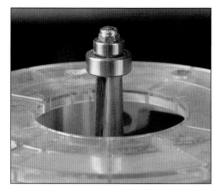

141. *For the first pass, place a 3/4 inch bearing on a 1/2 inch spiral router bit. For the second pass replace the 3/4 inch bearing with a 5/8 inch bearing.*

142. *Rout along the spline, being especially careful where the spline steps up to the breadboard end. End grain is exposed at this point, making blowout a concern.*

143. *After trimming, a point is formed at both ends, where the spline exits the groove. Both of these points must be relieved with a chisel because, with changes in humidity, the spline will move in and out of the groove on the breadboard-end side.*

144. *When relieving the point, be careful not to slip with the chisel and mark the top.*

145. *The finished breadboard detail with ebony spline.*

Once the glue is dry, set a router up with a 1/2 inch flush trimming spiral bit, but remove the 1/2 inch bearing and replace it with a 3/4 inch (oversize) bearing (**141**). Rout along the spline (**142**), being especially careful at the point of transition where the spline steps up to the bread board end. End grain is exposed at this point making blow out a concern. Exchange the 3/4 inch bearing for a 5/8 inch bearing and again rout the ebony spline.

Being careful not to slip and mar the edge of the top, with a very sharp chisel relieve the sharp "points" at either end of the spline (images **143** and **144**). Note that the "point" on the breadboard end side of the joint should be relieved right to the point of the spline cavity thereby allowing the spline to move inward when the core contracts.

The spline is a feature that begs the sensation of touch, and for this reason sanding to a velvety smooth feel is essential. Starting with 150-grit and working up to 400-grit sandpaper, ease the edges and sand the face of the spline. In this instance, buffing the spline prior to inserting it is not possible, but ebony sanded to 400-grit will have a nice warm glow when the topcoat of finish is applied (**145**).

146. *The Blacker House bookcase, c.1907 -09. A classic Greene & Greene design, this piece resides in the Nelson-Atkins Museum of Art, Kansas City, MO.*

The Nelson-Atkins Museum of Art, Kansas City, Missouri (Purchase: acquired through the generosity of Mr. and Mrs. R. Hugh Uhlmann) F91-23; photo by Robert Newcombe

147. *The Thorsen sideboard (c.1909-10) is a Greene & Greene masterpiece! It resides at the Huntington Library in San Marino, California.*

Ognan Borisov/ Interfoto

Chapter 14
Pulls and Hardware

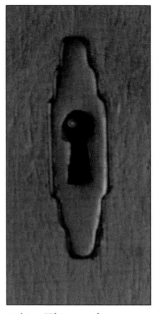

148. *This wooden escutcheon was made for a door in the Thorsen House living room.*

149. *The adjustable shelf system for the Robinson House relied upon a long, thin shelf support, rounded on both ends to fit in like-shaped slots.*

Gustav Stickley designed hand-hammered copper hardware, which was produced by craftsman in his own shop. For Stickley, there was a fundamental reason for this approach: it was at the heart of his Arts and Crafts philosophy, which placed a higher value on skilled work by the human hand than the mindless production of a machine. Stickley wrote, "When we come to make things ourselves and because they are needed, instead of depending on the department store to furnish them, we shall not only find pleasure in making them, but we shall also take more pleasure in possessing them."

Charles and Henry, being influenced by Stickley and the Arts and Crafts Movement, had a similar point of view, but with a different flavor. Unlike Stickley, and possibly because of their close relationship with the Halls, almost all of the Greenes' shop-made hardware was produced from wood. As they had done with joinery, the Greenes transformed the visible hardware items such as pulls and escutcheons into simple but elegant works of art. Henry Greene wrote, "The idea was to eliminate everything unnecessary, to make the whole as direct and simple as possible, but always with the beautiful in mind as the first goal."

It is unclear who specifically designed individual pieces of Greene & Greene hardware. It is likely, though, that Charles designed the pulls and escutcheons, and that Henry, with his mechanical aptitude, most likely designed the mechanisms for drop front desks and dining table extensions. Some things, such as drawer runners and adjustable shelf mechanisms, may have originated with the Halls.

Greene & Greene typically used wooden runners mounted beneath the drawer. This was most definitely a detail in which Charles and Henry were involved. Text from a typical Greene & Greene contract regarding the built-in drawers reads: Drawers: throughout to have oak center guide. large drawers in closet to be fitted with two guides each. (Metal drawer slides were not available at the time the Halls were building Greene & Greene furniture, and at any rate, with beauty in mind as the first goal, it is highly unlikely they would have used such slides if they could.)

The Hall brothers used at least two different methods for adjustable shelves. In the Robinson House (**149**) they relied upon a long, thin piece of wood, rounded on both ends to fit in a series of like-shaped slots, with the shelf resting on top of the fitted wooden piece. For the Thorsen House (**119** page 72) a series of holes were drilled in a zigzag pattern, but instead of a metal pin they used a hand carved piece of wood with a dowel-shaped end as the adjuster.

It was quite common in the time of Charles and Henry for escutcheons to be manufactured items—either thin metal overlays or small metal inserts. However, wooden, and often inlayed, escutcheons were the standard fare for Greene & Greene furniture and built-ins. There is a special delight that comes with discovering a would-be insignificant detail, such as a escutcheon, that is not only hand made with wood, but has been intricately inlaid into the door or drawer as well (**148** and **152**).

150. *A simple but effective pull from the right-side door of the Thorsen sideboard. Notice the inlaid ebony escutcheon just to the left.*

151. *A wooden pull from the Robinson House built-in bookcase. This is one of the Greenes' first collaborations with the Hall brothers.*

152. *At first glance this pull and escutcheon appear to be made of a dark metal. It is a pleasant surprise to discover they are individually carved from wood.*

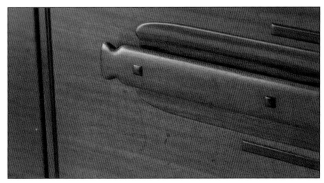

153. *This pull is from a lower drawer of the Thorsen House living room bookcase. Although its design is simple and straightforward, considerable labor was involved in its construction.*

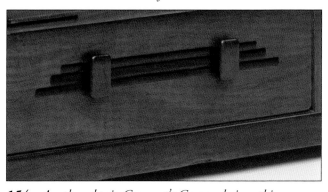

154. *Another classic Greene & Greene design, this complex pull is from the lower drawer of the bookcase from the Blacker House living room.*
The Nelson-Atkins Museum of Art, Kansas City, Missouri
(Purchase: acquired through the generosity of Mr. and Mrs. R. Hugh Uhlmann)
F91-23; photo by Robert Newcombe

Greene & Greene pulls were never stock items merely supplied from a catalog or by a vendor. From the beginning, their pulls were frequently designed for a particular piece, or limited group, of furniture. Some pulls, such as used for the Blacker and Gamble Houses, were quite involved (see **146** and **154**).

Simpler pulls found on the furniture of the Thorsen dining room (images **150** and **147**) represent a variant of what might be called the standard Greene & Greene pull, and variations of it may be found throughout the brothers' careers on many pieces of furniture. Greene & Greene pulls were always shop made and, with the exception of perhaps just one pull used in the Bush and Gamble furniture, did not contain any metal parts. Even when the design of a pull would have been well suited for

metal, wood was still chosen. A good example of this is the pulls on the cabinets from the Fleishhacker game room (**152**), which at first glance appear to be a very dark metal, but upon closer examination are indeed proven to be carved wood.

The Blacker House living room pull (**154**) will be our focus in this chapter. This pull represents classic Greene & Greene at its best! It is a beautiful and imaginative solution that invites the hand to interact; and as often was the case, it was used for just the one room of one project and never used again. It consists of three proud ebony bars and a rectangular-shaped block placed atop the bars. The backside of the block is cove-shaped, creating a comfortable place for the fingers to grasp.

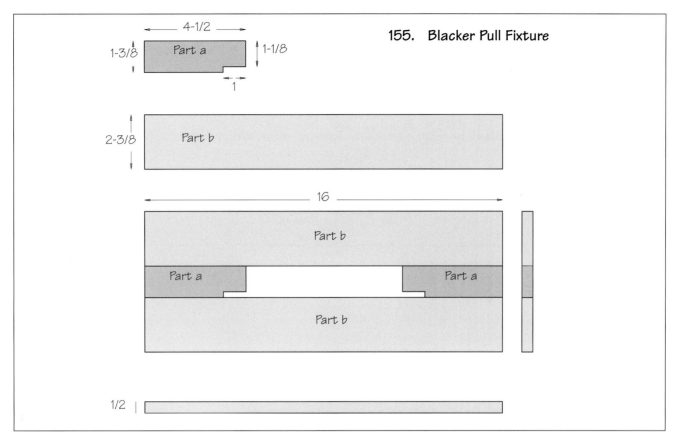

155. Blacker Pull Fixture

Making the Routing/Insert Fixture

The construction of the Blacker House pull (**154**), despite its simple appearance, presents the furniture maker with several problems. The pull or knob itself is a relatively easy matter, but the ebony bars call for precise work. A fixture for routing out the cavity for the ebony bars is the first order of business. The fixture is essentially a flat board with an opening for three different size inserts—a specific insert for each of the bars. The fixture and its inserts must be very precise if the bars are to fit properly. To make the fixture body, cut two pieces of 1/2 inch MDF at 1-3/8 by 4-1/2 inches (part a), and two pieces at 2-3/8 by 16-3/16 inches (part b). As seen in drawing **155**, the smaller two pieces (part a) each have a 1/4 by 1 inch notch in one of their inside corners.

Leaving a 7-3/16 inches space

156. *The holding fixture for the Blacker House living room pull is assembled with biscuits. See drawing **155**.*

between the two smaller pieces, align them between the two larger pieces and mark for biscuits or small dowels (**156**). Then join them together. After glue-up, mark the centers of the insert openings on all four interior edges, this will be used later to center stock (drawer front) on the jig.

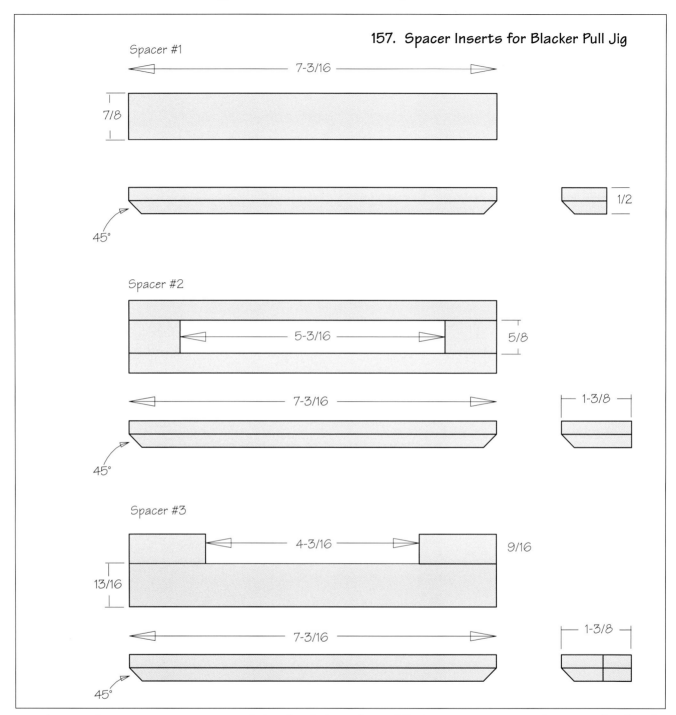

157. Spacer Inserts for Blacker Pull Jig

Spacer #1

7-3/16

7/8

45°   1/2

Spacer #2

5-3/16   5/8

7-3/16   1-3/8

45°

Spacer #3

4-3/16   9/16

13/16

7-3/16   1-3/8

45°

Making the Inserts

All inserts are 1/2 inch thick (**157**). Insert number one produces the longest bar at the bottom, and is a simple rectangle measuring 7/8 inch by 7-3/16 inches, with the bottom chamfered on the three sides that go against the insert opening. Insert number two is for the middle bar and has a finished size of 1-3/8 by 7-3/16 inches, with a 5/8 inch by 5-3/16 inches hole in the middle. To construct insert number two, join the two centerpieces measuring 5/8 by 1 inch to the longer outside pieces measuring 3/8 inch by 7-3/16 inches, leaving an opening in the middle that is 5/8 inch by 5-3/16 inches. It may be easier to make all the pieces longer, and then trim them to overall length after the glue-up, while making certain the whole remains exactly centered. Chamfer all four bottom outside edges. Insert number three is for the topmost bar and is a simple rectangle measuring 1-3/8 by 7-3/16 inches, with a 9/16 inch high by 4-3/16 inch notch out of the exact middle of the top edge. The notch can be cut out with repeated passes of a dado head or glued up from individual pieces as insert number 2 was.

158. *The fixture with spacer number one inserted in its correct position. The slots seen at the top of the insert, at either side of the template opening, are for prying the insert out.*

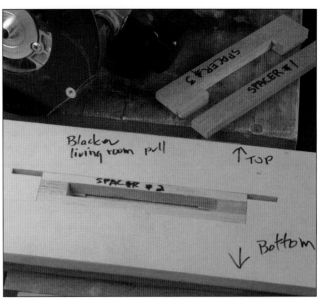

159. *The fixture with spacer number two inserted in its correct position. The inserts should fit snug but not tight.*

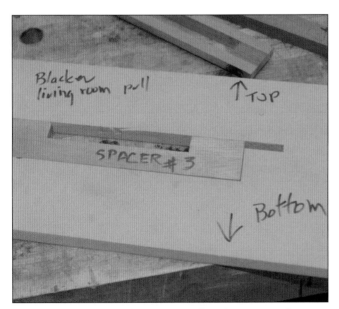

160. *The fixture with spacer number three inserted in its correct position. It is important that both the holding template and insert spacers be made precisely to size.*

161. *Rout out the cavity for the ebony bars with a plunge router. If chips and debris clog the working area, stop routing and blow them clear.*

Routing the Cavity for the Bars

To use the bar routing fixture, first setup a plunge router with a 1/2 inch collar and a 3/8 inch down spiral bit. Set it to cut 1/16 inch deep (1/16 inch into the stock— that is 1/16 inch past the bottom side of the fixture). Draw centerlines on the drawer front representing the location of the pull, align them with the centerlines on the template, and clamp in place. Orient the individual inserts one at a time (**158**, **159**, **160**, **161**) in the fixture opening, and rout out a cavity for the three ebony bars. The notch that was made in the fixture body (part a) can be used in conjunction with a narrow screwdriver to pry the tight fitting inserts out.

162. *The ebony bar stock is pillowed, then progressively sanded to 400-grit. The bar is then buffed with a white abrasive pad. The bar shown here is extra long—it has not yet been cut to length.*

163. *A radius guide (drafting tool) is used to mark out the appropriate radius on the end of each bar.*

Making the Bars

For your first time making the ebony bars, it may be prudent to run through the process with scrap material. Then, once the accuracy of the fixture and inserts are established, make the bars in ebony. To make the bars, mill one piece of ebony stock to 3/8 inch x 7-1/8 inches, plus another to 3/8 inch x 4-1/8 inches, and a third to 1/2 inch x 5-1/8 inches. The width of the stock is unimportant because multiple individual bars will be ripped from this stock. The top and the bottom bars are to be made from the 3/8 inch material with the middle bar coming from the 1/2 inch material. Pillow one face edge on each of the pieces of stock and ease the edges by hand sanding, starting with 120-grit sandpaper and changing to progressively finer grits until 400-grit is reached. Buff with a super fine grade of synthetic steel wool—000 or 0000 (**162**).

On the table saw, with a zero clearance throat plate, a wooden push stick, and using a rip blade, rip an 1/8 inch (pillowed) strip off each of the pieces of stock. Ripping narrow stock can be dangerous, make sure no one or anything important is directly behind the ripping operation. The zero clearance throat plate is a must for safety. If this procedure feels unsafe, find help to complete the operation. Holding the bar stock up to their respective openings, pencil mark their individual lengths and creep up on the final length with the aid of an edge or disc sander.

When routing out the drawer front, the 3/8 inch router bit left a 3/16 inch radius at the end of the cavity for each bar. The longest (bottom) bar has a fully formed 3/16 inch radius on its end. The other two bars have ends that on one side die into the adjoining bar. Depending on the accuracy of the jig and other variables, the end radii on the two upper bars may not be fully-formed. Whatever the situation, the bars

164. *Using a sanding block with 120-grit sandpaper, blend the end radius to its final shape.*

165. *This is the bottom bar:*

need to be individually fit to their respective locations. Using a plastic radius guide (available at an office supply store), mark out the appropriate 3/16 inch radius on the ends of each of the bars (**163**). Using a disc or edge sander, carefully waste away the small amount of material outside the line, but do not try to give the radius its final shape. Blend the pillowed shape with the end radius to final shape by hand with a sanding block and 120-grit sandpaper, again working up to finer grades of sandpaper (**164** and **165**). Ease and buff the radiused end of the bar.

Final Fitting and Gluing the Bars

The bars are now ready to dry fit as a whole (**166**). Should they fail to fit precisely on the first try, there are two remedies. If the dimension of the bars can be altered in a minor way so that it doesn't change the perceptible appearance of the overall pull detail, do that; otherwise the template or its inserts will need to be adjusted accordingly to correct the problem. Even when the sizing of the template and the bars are acceptable there may still be times when the bars fit just a hair too snug—in this case, with a small hand plane held stationary (**167**), take the last bar down in size until it fits properly. Once a good fit is achieved, spread a thin layer of glue in the bar cavity. Gently tap the bars in place using a small plastic headed mallet. Place the entire drawer front in a vice with wooden jaw faces and clamp the bars in place. If the drawer front is larger than the vice, simply clamp the drawer front between two flat boards.

166. *The finished ebony bars are ready for a final fitting before being glued into place.*

167. *If the fit is a bit too snug, hold a small hand plane stationary and use it to take the last bar down in size until it fits properly.*

Making the Pull

The next step is to machine the pull itself. Mill a small block of mahogany to 11/16 inch thick by 1-5/16 inches wide by 1-7/8 inches long (with the grain). Set up a 5/8 inch diameter core box bit in a router table to a height of 1/2 inch with the fence adjusted for a cutting depth of about 5/16 inch. Both the fence and the table throat must be zero clearance. Fashion a small piece of wood into a handheld hold-down. Run the pull blank through the router table set-up with a block of wood as a backup and using the handheld hold down (**168**). Mark approximately a 1/4 inch radius on

168. *A 5/8-inch diameter core box bit set in a router table is used to rout the finger pull on the backside of the pull. Fashion a small hold-down and back up the cut with a block of wood.*

all four corners of the face of the pull. Band saw to just outside the line and feather in the rounded corners with 120-grit sandpaper by hand (**169**). With a small hand plane and the pull held fast in a vice, rough out a pillowed shape on its face (**170**). Blend the roughed-out pillowed face with 120-grit sandpaper on top of a soft spongy surface (**171**). Round over the back edge of the face with sandpaper and sand all exposed surfaces of the pull to 220-grit.

The bars present a surface that is not flat. To give the pull a like-shaped mating surface, place a piece of 220-grit PSA (sticky back) sandpaper loosely over the bars. Position the pull on top of the sandpaper, aligning it to its proper relationship to the bars; evenly sand until the shape of the bars are transferred to the pull (**172**). The 220-grit sandpaper is chosen because it's paper is thin and conforms to the shape of the bars better. Be careful to sand evenly.

To mount the pull, mark and drill two 1/8 inch pilot holes in the bars. Counter-sink the drawer back for a number six wood screw. Attach the pull with two number 6 brass wood screws. And you're done (**173**).

169. *The rounded corners are first cut out on the band saw, and then blended to final shape by hand with 120-grit sandpaper.*

170. *With the pull held fast in a vice, roughly create a pillowed effect on its face with a small block plane.*

171. *With 120-grit sandpaper placed on top of a soft spongy surface, blend the roughed out face of the pull.*

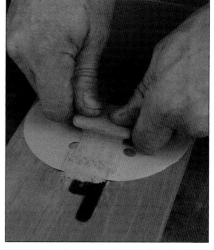

172. *To form the shape of the bars on the backside of the pulls, use a piece of 220-grit PSA (sticky back) sandpaper. Carefully conform the sandpaper to the shape of the bars. Then line up the pull and sand evenly until the shape of the bars are transferred to the pull.*

173. *The finished Blacker living room pull.*

Chapter 15
Proud Finger Jointed Drawers

A variety of joinery techniques for drawer construction can be found on Greene & Greene furniture. Some were simply half-lapped and doweled, while many employed a tongue-front joint (**175**). The Thorsen House furniture is perhaps the only Hall brothers/Greene & Greene furniture that features the dovetail joint (**176**).

In at least one instance from the Blacker House and in several examples from the Gamble House, the Greenes employed a proud exposed finger joint for drawer construction (**177**). The proud fingers are pillowed on the face and have rectangular ebony plugs placed between them. The fingers protrude further than the plugs do, so their degree of pillowing is greater.

This chapter will present a drawer joinery detail that is similar in character to, while not precisely representative of, the original Greene & Greene work. Original Greene & Greene finger joints had rectangular shaped ebony

plugs in-between each finger. If this feature is preferred, the drawer-fronts should be cut out with at least an inch of extra length at each end. After the mortises for the plugs have been machined and all danger of tear-out is passed, the drawer-fronts can then be cut to length.

The finger-jointing method presented here is certainly not the final word on the subject, so if the reader has an preferred method, by all means use it. This discussion will use, as a case in point, the drawer from the nightstand featured later in this book. Should the reader choose to build the nightstand there will also be included enough information to complete the drawer beyond the finger joint. Please be aware that the drawer construction presented is not typical of original Greene & Greene furniture, but nonetheless relies upon traditional joinery and is in the spirit of the original Greene & Greene work.

Cutting Out the Drawer Parts

To begin, cut out the solid wood parts for the drawer as per drawing **174** and the cut list given here, but leave the drawer-back about a quarter-inch long.

    Drawer front: 1 each 1/2 inch x 3 inches x 16 inches

    Drawer sides: 2 each 1/2 inch x 3 inches x 12-1/4 inches

    Drawer back: 1 each 1/2 inch x 2-1/2 inches x 15-1/2 inches

    Drawer bottom: (plywood) 1/4 inch x 10-3/8 inches x 15-7/16 inches

Also cut an extra front and side from scrap material to use for set-ups. Care must be taken to make all the parts flat and the drawer sides and front exactly the same width. The joinery will only be as good as the prep work: if the parts are not precise, neither will the joinery be.

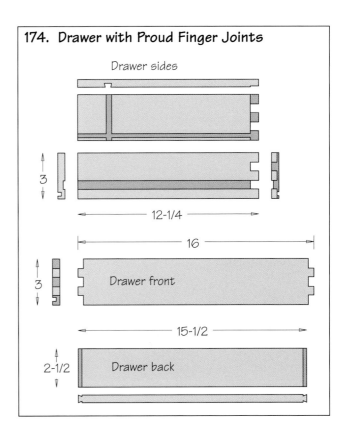

174. Drawer with Proud Finger Joints

Drawer sides

3

12-1/4

16

3

Drawer front

15-1/2

2-1/2

Drawer back

175. *A simple tongue front-joint from a Robinson House built-in drawer.*

176. *This is a dovetailed drawer from the Thorsen House living room. The Thorsen House is perhaps the only place where the Halls employed dovetails on Greene & Greene furniture.*

177. *The proud finger-joint shown here is from the Gamble House chiffonier. There is at least one instance from the Blacker House where the Greenes also employed a finger-joint for drawer construction.*

Making the Drawer-Front Fingers

Next set up a dado head in the table saw with about 1/2 inch width. Prepare a table saw sled with a piece of MDF to act as a zero clearance rear fence. Set the dado head in conjunction with the sled to make a 3/8 inch high cut. Set a stop (squared up block of wood) 5/8 inch from the far side of the dado head (**178**). Referring to image **179** for orientation, make the cut first in the scrap drawer-front with the stock up against the stop block, then a second cut spaced far enough away from the stop block to waste the remaining material (**180**). If the cut is correct within (five-thousandths inch, as measured with calipers, if available), repeat the cut on the other side of the test piece (**181**) repeat the entire sequence on both ends of the actual drawer-front. Make certain to save a scrap piece with the correct dado cuts for future use.

With the outside portion of the drawer-front-fingers now formed, using the same dado height, place the stop block so that when a pass is made from each side of the drawer-front the resulting cut in the middle will be 5/8 inch (**182**). Once the test piece yields the proper cut, do it again on both ends of the actual drawer-front. The drawer-front fingers are now done.

178. Set the dado head in conjunction with the sled to make a 3/8 inch high cut. Set a stop (squared up block of wood) 5/8 inch from the far side of the dado head.

179. First make the cut in the scrap drawer-front with the stock up against the stop block.

180. The second cut is far enough away from the stop block to waste the remaining material.

181. Once a successful cut is achieved on the scrap material, repeat the entire sequence on both ends of the actual drawer-front.

182. Using the same dado height, now position the stop block so that when a pass is made from each side of the drawer-front the resulting cut in the middle will be 5/8 inch. Once the test piece yields the proper cut, do it again on both ends of the actual drawer-front.

183. *Use the calipers to measure one of the fingers produced. If all the milling up to this point was fairly accurate the finger should measure 9/16 inch (.5625). The other finger should be exactly the same size. The corresponding fingers must now be cut into the drawer-sides, which will fill the negative space left by the draw-front fingers.*

184. *With the dado width properly established, run the dado height to 5/8 inch. For an initial positioning of the stop block, set the drawer-front in next to the stop block and move it over until the dado head lines up with the finger on the drawer-front.*

185. *With the test piece, run the cuts from both sides and check for a good fit with the drawer-front. The fingers should fit snug but not overly tight. The newly cut drawer-side fingers should be proud of the drawer front by 1/8 inch. Unless you are very lucky, there is likely to be some adjustment to get it correct.*

Making the Drawer-Side Fingers

Use the calipers to measure one of the fingers produced (**183**). If all the milling up to this point was fairly accurate the finger should measure 9/16 inch (.5625). The other finger should be exactly the same size. The corresponding fingers must now be cut into the drawer-sides, which will fill the negative space left by the draw-front fingers, and be proud of the drawer-front surface by 1/8 inch.

Take the dado head apart and, with shims, if necessary, set it to cut a width of 9/16 inch plus about 5 thousandths, or just the slightest hair over 9/16 inch. This measurement matches the width of the drawer-front fingers. If the drawer-front fingers came out to be something other than 9/16 inch, adjust the width of the dado to that number plus about five-thousandths. With the dado width properly established, set the dado height to 5/8 inch. This depth of cut should produce a finger that is proud of the drawer-front by 1/8 inch. For an initial positioning of the stop block, set the drawer-front in next to the stop block and move it over until the dado head lines up with the finger on the drawer-front (**184**). With the test piece, run the cuts from both sides and check for a good fit with the drawer-front (**185**). The fit should have just the slightest bit of resistance when pulling apart. If it is too tight or too loose, use the calipers to determine where it is off and make adjustments to either the position of the stop block or the width of the dado head accordingly. Once a suitable fit is achieved, run the actual drawer-sides, referencing from both sides to produce three fingers.

Machining the Dado for the Drawer Runner

Next, without changing the width of the dado, set its height to 1/8 inch. With the drawer-side against the rip fence, line up the dado head with the cut just made (**186**). This is the dado cut for the drawer runner. At this time it must be determined which of the drawer side parts will be rights versus lefts. Mark them as such, and also mark them for bottom and outside. With the bottom against the fence and the outside facing down, run the dado cut for the drawer runner in the sides (**187**).

186. *Without changing the width of the dado, set its height to 1/8 inch. With the drawer-side against the rip fence, line up the dado head with the cut just made. This is the dado cut for the drawer runner. The drawer-sides should be marked for right and left at this time, as well as for bottom and outside.*

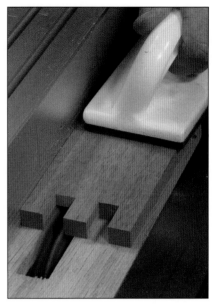

187. *With the bottom against the fence and the outside facing down, run the dado cut for the drawer runner in the sides.*

Finishing Off the Finger Joint

The finished fingers on the drawer-sides are 3/8 inch thick while the drawer-side stock itself is 1/2 inch thick, a difference of 1/8 inch. To take the fingers down to their correct thickness, leave the dado depth of cut at its present setting (1/8 inch), and set the stop block to the length of the fingers. In other words, when the drawer-side fingers are placed up against the stop block, the resulting cut would be even with the bottom of the negative space between the fingers (**188**).

Place the scrap drawer-side, with the inside facing down, and the fingers against the stop block. Make the cut and move the scrap drawer-side back from the stop block enough to remove the remaining material with the second pass. Check the test piece in the drawer-front for its fit. The fingers of the drawer-front should be fitting flush with the drawer-side, and the drawer-side fingers should be fitting without any visible gaps in the face of the drawer-front. The drawer side fingers should be 1/8 inch proud of the drawer-front surface. If the fit is not just right, make whatever appropriate adjustments are needed, test fit again and run the drawer-sides.

188. *The finished fingers on the drawer-sides are 3/8 inch thick, while the drawer-side stock is itself 1/2 inch thick, a difference of 1/8 inch. To take the fingers down to their correct thickness, leave the dado depth of cut at its present setting (1/8 inch), and set the stop block to the length of the fingers. In other words, when the drawer-side fingers are placed up against the stop block, the resulting cut would be even with the bottom of the negative space between the fingers. Again, use the scrap material from previous cuts to ensure the cut is correct and even with the bottom of the fingers.*

Cutting the Groove for the Drawer Bottom

Plywood is never its given 1/4 inch—it is always smaller—therefore it is necessary to make two passes with an 1/8 inch wide rip blade to produce a groove the actual width of the drawer-bottom.

Set the blade to a height of 1/8 inch. Set the rip fence to 1/4 inch and, placing the drawer-side (test piece) with the inside facing down and the bottom against the fence (**189**), cut a groove in the test piece as well as the actual drawer-side. With the inside facing down and the bottom against the fence, cut this groove in the drawer-front as well (**190**). With the calipers, measure the drawer-bottom material and adjust the rip fence to cut the additional width in the groove to accommodate the drawer-bottom. Test the cut on scrap material, then cut the actual parts.

189. *Set the blade to a height of 1/8 inch and set the rip fence to 1/4 inch. Place the drawer-side (test piece) with inside facing down and bottom against the fence, then cut a groove in the test piece as well as the actual drawer-side. With calipers, measure the drawer-bottom material. Adjust the rip fence so the groove will accommodate the drawer-bottom. Run the test piece first.*

190. *With the inside facing down and the bottom against the fence, machine the drawer's front at the same time as the drawer's sides.*

The Sliding Dovetail Back

Set up a router table with a 1/2 inch dovetail bit. Set the fence to 1-7/8 inches (back from the bit) and the height of the bit to 1/4 inch. With a piece of scrap, test the cut using a block of wood to back up the stock and prevent blowout. When the setup is correct, run the drawer-sides with the inside facing down and the back end of the drawer-side to the fence (**191**).

When the drawer sides are joined to the drawer-front, the distance between the two sides should be fifteen inches (if all the machining has been accurate up to this point). The drawer-back needs to be 1/2 inch longer than the distance between

the two sides. Cut the drawer-back to 15 1/2 inches long. If the distance between the sides is just a little off, adjust accordingly.

191. *Set up a router table with a 1/2 inch dovetail bit. Set the fence to 1-7/8 inches back from the bit and the height of the bit to 1/4 inch. Test the cut in scrap. using a back-up block to prevent blowout. When the setup is correct, run the drawer-sides with the inside facing down and the back end to the fence*

The Drawer Back – Sizing the Dovetail

Leaving the router bit height the same, set the router table fence for a very shallow cut and zero clearance. Make a test cut on both sides of scrap stock to form the dovetail shape (**192**). Test the resulting dovetail in the drawer-side, and then adjust the fence (depth of cut) accordingly. The dovetail should slide in without much resistance but still impart a small amount of friction.

Pillowing the Fingers

The exposed fingers now need to be sanded and pillowed. Take the scrap finger joint that was saved from the drawer-front machining and fit it to one of the drawer-sides. The fingers extending from the drawer-side can now be sanded and shaped without worry of scratching the actual drawer-front or removing too much material from the fingers. Ease all the edges of the fingers and pillow the faces by hand (**193**). With the exception of the outside faces of the drawer-sides, sand all the drawer parts to 220-grit.

Drawer assembly is easily accomplished in stages. For the finger joint glue-up, corner clamps are needed that allow for clearance of the proud fingers. Using two clamps per joint and checking for square, clamp and glue one corner at a time (**194**). Once the two sides and front are glued together, dry fit the drawer-bottom into its groove. If need be, adjust the height of the drawer-back so that when it is in place it's flush with both the drawer-bottom and the top of the drawer-sides. Glue the drawer-back in place. Check the drawer assembly for square. With a light bead of glue in the groove insert the drawer-bottom. If the drawer is

192. *Leaving the router bit height the same, set the router table fence for a very shallow cut and zero clearance. Make a test cut on both sides of scrap stock to form the dovetail shape. Test the resulting dovetail in the drawer-side, and then adjust the fence (depth of cut) accordingly. The dovetail should slide in without much resistance, imparting just a small amount of friction.*

193. *Take the scrap finger-joint that was saved from machining the drawer-front and fit it to one of the drawer-sides. The fingers extending from the drawer-side can now be sanded and shaped without worry of scratching the actual drawer-front or removing too much material from the fingers. Ease all the edges of the fingers and pillow the faces by hand.*

194. *Using two corner clamps and checking for square, clamp and glue one corner at a time.*

195. *The finished finger joint.*

slightly out of square it can be tweaked square by cross corner clamping. Once the drawer is truly square, run a liberal bead of hot melt glue along the bottom side of the drawer-bottom up against the drawer-sides and front. This keeps the

bottom from rattling and helps secure squareness.

The last step is to run two or three countersunk No. 6 x 1 inch brass screws from the bottom into the drawer back. The drawer is done (**195**).

Chapter 16
Greene & Greene Finishing

The finish Greene & Greene used for their furniture is not much of a mystery, as it can be pieced together by reviewing various historical documents. In the (Greene & Greene) Environmental Design Archives at U.C. Berkeley is a document spelling out very specifically the color formula for finishing the bedroom furniture of the William R. Thorsen House (1908 –1910):

Chemical Treatment: Bichromate of Potash, saturated solution. One part to four parts of water. Brush on and wipe off as work proceeds. One coat.

Filler/Stain:

Chrome Yellow L. 3-1/2 parts

Sylvan Green 1/8 part

Raw Umber 3 parts

White Lead 2-5/8 parts

Use 19 parts of raw oil with dryer. Wipe off.

After 48 hours rub in oil, wipe off thoroughly and polish with cheese cloth. After 48 hours repeat the last.

In documents found at the Huntington Greene & Greene archives in San Marino, California, the "raw oil" referred to is confirmed as being linseed oil. The following text is from an original Greene & Greene contract and is typical of wording found in many of their contracts pertaining to interior wood finish:

1st Treat chemically in two coats as directed. Allow time to dry as directed by architects, then sand lightly but evenly over whole surface with #00 sandpaper.

2nd Fill and stain as directed. When set wipe off with cheese cloth. Rub smooth and when thoroughly dry sand evenly over whole surface.

3rd After 48 hours brush on a coat of pure undiluted boiled linseed oil, wipe off until surface is per-

fectly dry, and then polish with woolen cloth to uniform surface.

4th When approved by architects, repeat coat of oil same as third.

The world of wood finishing has come a long way since the days of the Greenes and the Halls. Our purpose here is to present a method, taking advantage of safer modern materials, that will produce a comparable Greene & Greene look. But first, a finish is only as good as the sanding that preceded it, so before getting started, here are a few quick notes on sanding:

First, sand mahogany to 220-grit. Second, all parts should be fully sanded prior to assembly—it is very difficult to do a good job of sanding after a piece of furniture is built. Due to its very nature, there are bound to be small dents and scratches during the process of assembly, no matter how careful one is. It is much easier to deal with just a few dings and scratches later than it is to sand the entire project after assembly.

The finishing schedule presented here is one that has been found to work well, but is not the final word. Finishing wood is a never-ending search for refinement. Consider the following information a starting point.

Dyeing the Wood

As an alternative to the dangerous chemicals used by the Greenes and the Halls, and because of its light fastness and clarity, use a water-soluble aniline dye for altering the color of the wood, such as Liberon Brand English Brown Mahogany #43, available from Liberon/Star Wood Finish Supply. Our first step is to lightly sponge the wood with water to raise the grain, let it dry completely, then gently sand off the raised fibers with 320-grit sandpaper. This will prevent the grain from rising when the dye is applied.

The entire dyeing process is made easier by reducing the dye's strength and making two or three applications instead of just one. This not only gives you more control over the shade of color, but also helps cover up any irregularities caused by a single application. Using the Liberon dye #43, mix a one-ounce packet with distilled water as per the instructions on the package. Further reduce that with twelve parts distilled water to one part of the original dye mixture. Apply the dye with a terry cloth-covered sponge (**196**). With a little practice, the amount of dye being applied can be controlled with hand pressure. Each application should be fairly light. Be careful to provide an even application of dye and not flood the area. It is easy for wood to "wick-up" or pool in the corners and crevices if the surface is heavily flooded. Allow each application of dye to dry thoroughly and allow twelve to twenty-four hours before applying the top-coat.

It is difficult to gauge the darkness of the dye until the top-coat is applied. For that reason it is worthwhile to sand up four finish sam-

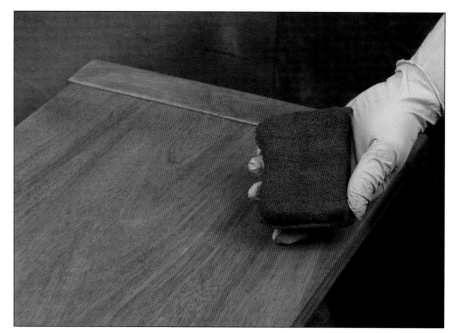

196. *Apply the dye with a terry cloth-covered sponge. With a little practice, the amount of dye being applied can be controlled by hand pressure.*

197. *Gauging the darkness of the dye can be difficult prior to the application of the top-coat. It is worthwhile to sand up four finish samples: apply two applications of dye on the first sample, and add an additional application of dye to each subsequent sample. Tape off half of each sample and apply topcoat to the un-taped half. Use the samples to gauge how dark the finish will be in relation to the unfinished dye.*

ples, apply two applications of dye on the first sample, and adding an additional application of dye to each subsequent sample. Tape off half of each sample and apply topcoat to the un-taped half. Use the samples to gauge how dark the fin-

ish will be in relation to the unfinished dye. The difference between a single application is slight (**197**), but the difference between two and five applications is discernable. Keep these samples for future reference.

Applying the top-coat

For the top-coat, there are numerous finishes on the market capable of producing a fine finish. The author has found General Finishes brand Arm-R-Seal Urethane Satin to produce excellent results. Arm-R-Seal is a brush-on wipe-off type finish. Apply four to six coats on a top surface and about three to five coats everywhere else. Achieving a high quality finish is time consuming—there just doesn't seem to be any way around it. Each coat must be applied and then wiped off just as it starts to become tacky. (Soft white cotton rags, available at any paint supply store, make ideal wiping cloths.) It is important to wipe off each coat thoroughly until, with a dry rag, no wet finish is picked up and the surface is totally dry (**198**). Then (and this is the time-consuming part) allow between 6 and 24 hours, depending on the temperature, between individual coats. If applied properly, the finish should start to show a nice sheen after three to four coats.

Applied finish will often work its way into nooks and crannies only to bleed out afterwards, leaving a run. To avoid this problem, use compressed air to blow out all the corners and adjoining surfaces (**199**). Normally, under average conditions, it will take about ten minutes for each of the first couple of coats to become slightly tacky, but in warm weather the finish will set up much faster, and in cooler conditions much slower. If the finish is left on too long it becomes difficult to remove. In this case re-apply fresh finish to loosen it up, then wipe off immediately. If the finish is removed too quickly it will take more coats to build to the desired sheen. As the

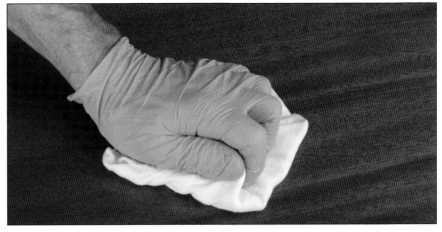

198. *Thoroughly wipe off each coat with a soft white cotton rag until no wet finish is picked up and the surface is completely dry.*

199. *Finish material bleeding out from nooks and crannies can ruin an otherwise beautiful finish. Blowing these areas out in advance can eliminate this problem.*

200. *A light buffing with the steel wool can remove most light smearing and streaking. For more stubborn situations, a reapplication of Bri-wax will dissolve the excess wax. To reduce the sheen left by the wax, buff again with 0000 steel wool.*

subsequent coats are applied and the finish starts to build it will begin to tack up much sooner. When this happens, the finish must be applied and removed in smaller sections at a time. (Remember, oily rags can spontaneously combust! To dispose of them properly, spread them flat and out-of-doors to dry.)

Bri-wax brand Antique Mahogany wax can be used after the final coat of Arm-R-Seal. Use #0000 steel wool to apply the wax, working it

into all the pores. If the wax is applied too heavily smearing and streaking will result. Most light smearing and streaking can be removed by a light buffing with the steel wool. For more stubborn situations, a reapplication of Bri-wax will dissolve the excess wax.

Finally, to reduce the high sheen left by the wax, again buff lightly with 0000 steel wool (**200**). Over time, as needed, the wax may be reapplied to freshen up the finish.

Chapter 17

Greene & Greene:
Striking Out On Your Own!

In the last several chapters we covered the construction of those details that comprise the Greene & Greene style. In this chapter we will discuss taking those details and assimilating them into one's own work. Furniture design is a large subject and it is not the purpose of this book to delve too deeply into the matter; however, we will briefly discuss a few important ideas and point the reader in the direction of further study.

Each person sees the world in a certain way, reflecting his or her own unique outlook on life. When Charles Greene developed his designs, he was doing more than engaging in a simple intellectual exercise of bringing together this or that detail. Charles was following a powerful vision. In Michael Crichton's book and movie Jurassic Park, the character Ian Malcolm, a mathematician, explains the chaos theory with the analogy of the "butterfly effect." The theory goes: "depending on whether a butterfly in Beijing flaps its wings, there is or is not rain in Central Park." Remove some small characteristic or event in the lives of Charles and Henry and their designs may well have turned out differently.

The Greene & Greene details together form a cohesive statement, and that statement is the expression of two people: Charles and Henry Greene. While we may find we relate to that statement on a deep level, when it comes right down to it, it is not our own statement. It is not our own creation. If we were to put forth our own statement in the form of a piece of furniture, what would it look like? How much or how little would we want to borrow from Greene & Greene? Are there other details from other sources that have caught our eye? There are a thousand different things we could do to "tweak" the design to make it more our own. The reader is greatly encouraged to use the building blocks put forth in the previous chapters to create his own offshoot of the Greene & Greene style.

Unlike the furniture of Gustav Stickley, Greene & Greene furniture was not mass-produced. The original Stickley furniture, now considered antiques, is relatively easy to obtain, and new pieces are being produced from the Stickley factory. Greene & Greene furniture on the other hand simply doesn't exist on the open market. It only survives in books and museums for us to see, and if the style is relegated to only being historical material it becomes stagnant and dies. For the Greene & Greene style to enjoy a vibrant future it must be made anew by contemporary craftsmen. The furniture designer/makers featured later in this book have done just that. They have taken the style and infused a bit of themselves into the mix, each creating something fresh and exciting, each coming at it from a different direction, and each having added something new to the Greene & Greene-inspired portfolio.

The world has changed immensely since the original Greene & Greene furniture was built. If Charles Greene were alive today it is most certain that he would be designing much different furniture. Today, furniture is called upon to serve purposes not even dreamed of one hundred years ago, when the Ultimate Bungalows were being built. Wouldn't it be interesting to see what Charles would have done had he been commissioned to design a media cabinet or a computer desk? Had the Greenes and the Halls been born one hundred years later, they would have grown up in a world with such things as particleboard and biscuit joiners. What materials and methods would be acceptable to them? Would they even be attracted to the revival of the American Arts and Crafts Movement, or would they be off on a different tangent? It is very likely if the Greenes were young architects in today's world, their designs would be unrecognizably different from the Greene & Greene style we know, but they would doubtless be designing masterpieces nonetheless.

The point is that the world has changed and the function of furniture has changed along with it. Even if our purpose is to faithfully re-create the Greene & Greene style, new problems and concerns must be addressed for the furniture to serve us well. In its renewal, the style must adapt to, and function well in, our contemporary world—it must discover its own natural path. In some instances it will no doubt be very much like the originals, and in other cases it will be greatly changed. It may also be that just one small detail, say the Blacker brackets, are picked up and used in a totally new style. Whatever the case, the Greene & Greene style then becomes a part of our culture, alive and well.

A person who truly wishes to emulate Charles Greene's approach to furniture design would do well to consider breaking the rules—just as Charles did. Stickley set the standard and made the rules when he designed his line of Arts and Crafts furniture. Charles took that standard and set of rules and used it as a starting point. He added to it, and subtracted from it, and tweaked it to suit himself.

Breaking the rules is a healthy act for any art form, and new styles would never exist if the rules were not broken. (Please note that by "rules" we do not mean those eternal rules of balance and proportion. They are here to stay and not paying attention to them is asking for serious trouble. Rather, we are speaking of sets of design features that are brought together to form a style.) In 1965 Bob Dylan plugged his guitar into an amplifier at the Newport Folk Festival. He broke the rules and was booed off the stage, but a new and vibrant form of folk music was brought to life. Just like Dylan, Stickley broke the rules in designing his own furniture, as did Stickley's predecessor and so on. So a part of truly emulating Charles Greene would be to break the rules: take the Greene & Greene style and go one's own direction, wherever that may be.

The motivation for a design can come from anywhere. For instance, it can be from nature: the cloud lift detail was said to be inspired by cloud formations. Objects seemingly unrelated to furniture such as the tsuba or Japanese sword guards are capable of motivating a design.

More often than not the design process is nothing more than a very small dose of inspiration combined with a whole lot of trial and error. Inspiration for creative works is sometimes not easily turned on. Often it comes uninvited, at unlikely places and on its own schedule. When a creative thought surfaces it is usually fleeting in nature and often ill-defined. It is prudent to commit the errant idea, no matter how vague, to some material form as soon as possible.

There are a number of methods that can aid in refining an idea once it is on paper or screen. Computer CAD programs have become indispensable aids in the creative process. A first rendition can be copied, then altered many time over and compared with the original in a very short time. No erasers or t-squares needed! And it's easy to produce a scale mock-up by laminating a drawing printout to foam core and cutting the parts out with a sharp knife.

Sometimes you may find a design in a book that gives you much inspiration, and you aspire to emulate it. Here is a method that sometimes works to trick the mind into being creative, that gets to the essence of an inspiring design. Take the design in question and study it closely for a few minutes every evening. After a couple of weeks, when its image is etched into your brain, close the book and put it away. Think about the design every day for a few minutes and try to imagine what it is that first attracted you to it—but do not refer back to the design itself. After a couple of weeks of this, draw the design from memory only. It is unlikely that your drawing will precisely match that from the book. It may, in fact, morph into something quite different and lead to new and interesting things.

If you have an idea for a design in the form of a drawing, but it is not quite hitting the mark, keep that drawing in front of you where it can be seen everyday, several times a day (such as a refrigerator door). Look at it; take notes, or sketch on it; continue refining it until it more clearly defines the original inspiration.

Creativity comes in many forms, and there is a lot to be said in favor of faithfully reproducing an existing design. The process of woodworking is itself challenging and quite capable of providing all the creativity we need. Woodworking is akin to problem solving, and therein lays the creativity, for creativity is at its best when it solves a difficult construction problem.

Without the Henry Greenes of the world, the Charles Greenes would not survive. While Henry was certainly a competent designer, his true talent and creative nature resided in organization and things mechanical. There is a special satisfaction that comes when all the different parts of a complex project come together and fit as planned. The sense of accomplishment derived from seeing a completed piece of furniture in front of you, one created by your own hands that required special skills and knowledge, is truly very rewarding.

Sometimes a particular furniture design speaks to us in a special way. In making a replica of such a piece of furniture, especially one that has as many subtle details as Greene & Greene designs often do, we become acutely aware of the nuance of play and interplay within the design. We learn something of the designer's original intentions, and in the process learn something of our own likes and dislikes.

Time Honored Rules of Design

Good proportioning and balance are ingredients common to all good designs, no matter what the style. There are countless methods, some quite ancient, that profess to hold the key to good design. The golden rectangle or, as it is sometimes called, the golden section, is probably the best known of the proportioning methods. Examples of the golden rectangle are replete in nature, and throughout the ages many works of art and architecture have conformed to the golden rectangle. It may be, though, that many of these compliant examples were not intentional. Their designers may have developed over time an innate ability to feel or sense good proportioning and balance. There is a primal attraction in the deep bass rhythm of the human heartbeat that perhaps comes from our unconscious sense of security in our mother's womb. Perhaps it is some similar primal appeal that attracts us to the ratio of 1:1.618, which makes up the golden rectangle.

The golden rectangle can be a bit esoteric though, and its practical application unclear for the casual user. A more practical source of study for balance and proportion is William H. Varnum's book Industrial Arts Design, A Textbook of Practical Methods for Students, Teachers, and Craftsman. Originally published in 1916, the book was republished in 1995 by Gibbs-Smith as Arts and Crafts Design. Varnum gets right to the point with practical, easy-to-understand applications. He seems to have an acute "feel" for balance and proportion and does not rely upon historical methods or formulas, instead creating his own set of rules. Whatever the system or recipe for good design, there must be some inspiration behind it all or the work may suffer and become bland and sterile.

It is a primary purpose of this book to promote the assimilation of the Greene & Greene style into new works in the hope that the style will continue to flourish. The reader is encouraged to take the information contained in the previous chapters and use it as a painter uses paint from their pallet. Mix the details of Greene & Greene as you will to your own liking. The following chapters contain examples from contemporary Greene & Greene style furniture makers, each with his own unique perspective on the style. They are here to point the way.

201. *Arnold d'Epagnier's dining room cabinet—a creative blend of Greene & Greene elements with other motifs.*

Arnold d'Epagnier

Chapter 18
Arnold d'Epagnier, Furniture Designer

My personal goal as a participant in the Arts and Crafts movement is to provide new designs that relate to the Mission Style—I want to keep the style alive and exciting, dovetailing with current lifestyles while not reproducing the past. Furniture design must change with the needs of the customer.

My new forms and designs are inspired by all of those past artisans, working around the turn of the 20th century, who sought to create beauty by hand-making an object, and by being in touch with the natural world and its simple pleasures. I attempt to orchestrate their artistic details into works of art, creating unique furnishings that add to the Arts and Crafts movement (**202**).

After 28 years of making furniture as art, my designs still use the philosophies of Arts and Crafts and Greene & Greene as their foundations. I develop my furniture designs by selectively arranging a few representative details. For example, one detail is inspired by Gustav Stickley's chairs that use functional, repetitive, uniform vertical strips of wood. Another detail is inspired by the arch used by Charles Rennie Mackintosh; in the entrance to the Glasgow School of Art one can see his superb use of many gentle arcs to make an otherwise flat wall into a work of art. Greene & Greene's cloud lift is yet another such detail. Although the designs that evolve from these points of inspiration may appear very different from the originals, by using representative details a historical link is maintained. This is evolution.

Dining Room Cabinet

The inspiration for this piece came to me while viewing the seashore near the James House, designed by the Greene brothers. I wanted to do the work they did so badly that I could feel it in all my senses. At first I thought I should just start reproducing their works, even though I'd never get their same ambiance and quality.

202. *Mirror vanity with Greene & Greene influence.*
Arnold d'Epagnier

Then I realized, in a spiritual type moment as the waves crashed and a dark storm approached, that they were inspired by what surrounded them, and that is the essence of art. I decided that I would do the same.

I am from Maryland, inland from the Atlantic Ocean—nothing like the spectacular west coast and its many beauties! So at home in Maryland I searched for its representative beauties. In my work I try to send the message that Arts and Crafts can be found wherever you look for it. I have always found the abundance of Black-Eyed Susan flowers, the Maryland State flower, pleasing and cheerful. I try to interpret and present them as an Arts and Crafts motif. I have also found subtle inspiration from memories of my youth, such as the peaceful visits to the estate where my architect father, the son of a horseman/chauffeur, grew up—cool memories of sipping iced tea while being surrounded by large boulders and a babbling brook. My work in Arts and Crafts has been influenced by these things.

Dining Room Cabinet

The dining room cabinet (**201**) is inspired by Greene & Greene's chiffonier found in the Gamble House master bedroom. It is my third version, where the first is a woman's wardrobe, and the second is a TV entertainment center. Both are seen on my website. I combined design details from several Arts and Crafts artisans. The overhanging top has the feel of Charles Rennie Mackintosh. The Greenes are represented in several cloud lifts throughout, along with the proud rolled-finger joints. The inclusion of marquetry is due to my admiration of Harvey Ellis. Function and simplicity of course reflect on Stickley. A modern day furniture artisan, James Krenov, has influenced me to select and place wood grains to compliment the whole three dimensional piece (**203**).

The marquetry is a stylized Arts and Craft

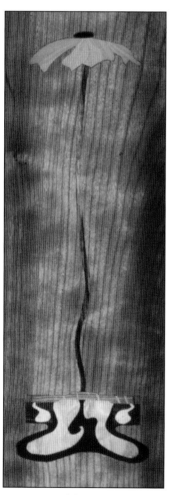

203. *Arnold's Black-Eyed Susan inlay shows an Art Nouveau influence.*
Arnold d'Epagnier

Black-Eyed Susan rising from an art nouveau foundation. That theme of black-eyed Susan is repeated in the silhouette of the pediment above the top—which is also shaped as a Greene & Greene cloud lift of waves (as per the Greenes' Fleishhacker House). The flower's silhouette appears again in a negative space in the top door stiles. It is reminiscent of the drooping petals during the hot humid Maryland August. It then metamorphoses into an art nouveau female profile with suggestive curves in silhouette. Wood grain patterns throughout are specifically chosen to direct the eye toward the pleasurable artistic features. The lower drawers have a zigzag grain pattern leading up to the central circular grain pattern in the middle drawers. Sides and back are done the same way using book match grain patterns. The close up of the Black-Eyed Susan shows Arts and Crafts style represented in the stem growing from an art nouveau foundation.

Sideboard

The sideboard (**205** and **206**) is a horizontal version of the dining room cabinet. Three utensil drawers form the top horizontal row. The central drawer is part of an overlay floral sculpture that continues as a stem into a pair of doors located below. This floral design is similar to an Arts and Crafts wallpaper motif. My "Maryland Arts and Crafts" look is seen in the marquetry of my state flower—the Black-Eyed Susan. The sideboard side panels show the actual flower. The front central doors show a Seccionist version and are flanked by small (square) doors in an Arts and Crafts version of the "four square" pattern.

Writing Desk

This is a desk (**207**) as I imagined might have been designed for the first users of the newly invented telephone. It has an overall Greene & Greene influence, but I made it asymmetrical, something that Charles would have played with eventually (but in a more astoundingly elegant way).

204. *Arnold d'Epagnier.*

205. *Arnold d'Epagnier's sideboard.*

Arnold d'Epagnier

206. *Sideboard (end view) with Black-Eyed Susan inlay.*

Arnold d'Epagnier

207. *A writing desk as might have been designed for the first users of the newly-invented telephone.*

Arnold d'Epagnier

208. *The Anderson server was influenced by the Blacker House desk (shown here with the Strand side chair).*

Thomas Stangeland

Chapter 19

Thomas Stangeland: Artist and Craftsman

The Influence of Greene & Greene

I was drawn to the Arts and Crafts movement in a different way than most of my fellow artisans. My early influences came from Art Deco and the Modernism movement. I loved combining sumptuous materials to create flamboyant statements. With little exposure to Arts and Crafts, I tended to think of it as heavy and dark. It was a customer's admiration of my work that prodded me into my first Greene & Greene commission. He sent me a photo of the Blacker House Armchair and asked me to build a set of eight. I leapt at the opportunity, as daunting a project as it was.

I began researching the chair through books and articles. I contacted The Huntington Library, which holds the Greene & Greene archives, though they refused to lend any help or assistance in ascertaining any dimensions. I relied upon the four or five images I could find and lofted the proportions of the chair with common sense. Little did I know this did not apply! I used proportions that related to people in the late-20th century. People at the dawn of the century were a bit smaller, as is the authentic Blacker Armchair.

This project taught me many of the fundamentals and fine points of building in the Arts and Crafts style, and of the nuance that Greene & Greene added. Pegged joints, mortise and tenons, and inlay were common to all Arts and Crafts designs. The Greene brothers' designs brought a soft subtlety and lightness to a style that was dominated by sharp and heavy structure. The introduction of the Asian influence gave rounded edges and broken lines through use of the cloud lift. I discovered all of these things and more from this first commission. It was an entirely new design lexicon that fascinated me.

After completing the chairs, I went on to build a dining table and sideboard for the same client. This commission generated further commissions, which led to desk designs and bedroom furniture. While reluctant at the onset, my path in this style was becoming clear. I knew from the beginning that I did not want to limit my work to reproductions. While my Blacker Arm and Side Chairs are not exactly authentic, they were intended to be. That was not the case with my other designs (**208** and **209**).

My goal was to adopt the design language of Greene & Greene and expand it into a series of contemporary works. The Arts and Crafts Bed (**214**) is an early example. Completely recognizable as Greene & Greene-inspired, it bears no specific resemblance to anything they created. In the instance of the Anderson Server, I seized upon one specific design element from the Blacker House Desk to create something different in scale and function (**210** and **211**).

To better understand the elements of Greene & Greene, I began to learn about their influences. Both the Japanese and Chinese cultures appear in the warp and weave of their designs. This became apparent in my work with the

209. *The Strand armchair is a fine example of a contemporary Greene & Greene inspired design.*

Thomas Stangeland

210. *Influences from both the Japanese and Chinese cultures are apparent in the Pyramid bench.*   Thomas Stangeland

211. *The reverse tapered leg on Tom's fused-glass table offers the eye a sense of lightness as it travels visually from bottom to top.*
Thomas Stangeland

212. *Thomas Stangeland's pyramid leg table is a wonderful blend of Chinese, Japanese, Art Deco, and Greene & Greene influences.*

Thomas Stangeland

Pyramid Leg Table (**215**), Fused Glass Table and the Pyramid Bench. All of these pieces rely on strong horizontal elements and heavy legs that root them to the ground. The reverse tapers offer the eye lightness as you travel visually from bottom to top. The Pyramid Leg Table also utilizes some of my more prized and exciting woods. While still bordered by long straight-grained timbers, the fields of the tabletops offer the opportunity to indulge my early Art Deco tendencies by using highly figured woods and inlay patterns.

214. *Thomas Stangeland's Arts & Crafts bed exemplifies a splendid use of Greene & Greene inspired details.*

Thomas Stangeland

213. *Thomas Stangeland.*

It's hard to guess where this style is going. One thing is certain: it's alive and evolving. I am one of many artisans who work in this design language. We all grow and continually come up with unique projects. Our inspirations may be the same; the similarities usually end there.

215. *Darrell Peart's Aurora table desk blends strong Greene & Greene influences with details from James Krenov and Seattle's Aurora bridge.*

216. *The drawers of the Aurora pedestal desk are defined by the arch passing through them.*

Chapter 20
Darrell Peart: Furniture Maker

As a furniture maker, I have had a variety of influences. Early on, I was inspired by the simple but elegant work of James Krenov. I read all his books, and attended his workshops and lectures when I could. The influence of Krenov can still be seen in my designs today. Gothic furniture appealed to me as well. I love the linenfold panels, the tracery, the pierced carvings and the bold masculine proportions. My initial impression was that Chippendale furniture is too busy and frilly. I still think that; however, when you strip away all the foo-foo, the balance and proportion is masterfully done! I gladly list Thomas Chippendale as an influence.

I first became aware of Greene & Greene through Alan Marks' superb 1978 article in Fine Woodworking Magazine. That first encounter left a positive impression, but at the time I remained firmly under the spell of Krenov. Several years later I was re-introduced to Greene & Greene and the Arts and Crafts Movement while working at a custom shop in Seattle. We had contracted to build some tables and display cases in the Arts and Crafts style. My co-worker was a passionate follower of the Arts and Crafts Movement and a confirmed fan of Greene & Greene. The project, however, was a farce. The "through tenons" were merely pasted on medallions and most of the material was veneered particleboard—including the legs! This was too much for my co-worker to bear, and as we progressed through the job he gave me a running commentary on the Arts and Crafts movement and a re-introduction to Greene & Greene. Up until this point I had only been aware of the Arts and Crafts Movement in a peripheral sort of way. I was struck by the similarity between the movement's philosophy and Krenov's approach to woodworking. It was this second, closer look at Greene & Greene that finally hooked me.

The work of Greene & Greene has had a most profound effect upon me. Their designs possess a sensitivity equal to that of Krenov and a sense of balance and proportion equal to that of Chippendale. Time and again I am amazed at the small subtle details that often go unnoticed in Greene & Greene designs. In the commercial cabinet shops where I have worked there is a quality standard concerning visual defects: if you cannot see the defect from x number of feet away, it should not be considered a defect. The reverse is true of Greene & Greene furniture: if you fail to get close enough you will miss much of the design.

Recently my wife and I visited the Los Angeles County Art Museum where the Blacker Living Room Desk was on display. This piece has long been a favorite design of mine, but I had only seen it in photos. I was awestruck—seeing it in real time was every bit as exciting as seeing the Beatles perform live when I was fifteen years old. I found a spot in front of the desk, as close as I could get without the guard becoming nervous, and stared myself into a stupor. I simply needed to feel it in my bones.

As a woodworker it is natural that I look upon joinery with a certain amount of fascination. I see joinery as something of beauty. But Greene & Greene took joinery's visual appeal to a new level. They didn't just celebrate its utilitarian nature, they transformed it into art itself, and in so doing appealed to those who don't have the faintest idea, nor care, what a breadboard or spline joint is. There is a part of me separate from the woodworker that takes great pleasure in a van Gogh or Seurat painting. It's that part of me as well as the woodworker that is attracted to Greene & Greene's use of joinery as art.

But it's more than the design work that attracts me to Greene & Greene. The Hall brothers, who built the furniture, were the ultimate craftsmen. I don't think the Greene's furniture would be as well-known today if not

217. *The Aurora nightstand is not a design that shouts for attention. Its appeal is simple yet quietly pleasing.*

for the superb craftsmanship of those in the Hall shop. The Gods were smiling upon earth when the Greene and the Hall brothers teamed up.

Greene & Greene's designs have affected me more than any other, but I don't feel bound to design strictly within their language. I like to draw from any source that appeals to me. I find that a design can only take you so far intellectually. It is ultimately an emotional thing: something that must be felt in my bones. My bones like Greene & Greene!

The Aurora Table Desk

218. *The Aurora Bridge in Seattle was in part the inspiration for both the Aurora table desk and Aurora pedestal desk.*

The Aurora Table Desk (**215**) is the first in a series of pieces with a slow graceful arch moving through the design. The arch came to me one day as I was standing in line at a grocery store in Seattle. Through the overhead window I could see the paired structural legs connected by graceful arches of the Aurora Bridge (**218**). The paired legs reminded me of the Blacker House living room table, which has four sets of paired legs. A single arch on the bridge would begin and end between each pair of legs. I liked both the idea of the paired legs and the arch. With my Aurora Table Desk the arch passes through the legs and as it does defines the shape of the drawers.

The term "Led Zeppelin" (as in the rock-n-roll group) has long held an attraction for me. It is a bit of an oxymoron, in that something can be light as well as heavy at the same time. That is how I perceive my table desk: light but stout (heavy). The four sets of paired legs and the proportioning of the negative space lends a certain stoutness to the design. However the desk does not have much in the way of mass, which ultimately lightens the design up considerably.

Aurora Pedestal Desk

A client liked my Aurora Table Desk, but needed more drawer space. The Aurora Pedestal Desk was the resulting design (**216**). As with the table desk, the arch in this piece defines the shape of the drawers as it passes through them, but in this case there are drawers on the bottom side of the arch as well. The bottom drawer is for files. I normally do not use European hardware but in this instance, because they are more practical, I used heavy-duty full extension slides. To accommodate the slides in a drawer design that did not have an overhanging front, I made the drawer sides 13/16 inch thick, which allowed me to recess the slides in a dado. Possessing the mass that the Table Desk lacks, this design is decidedly more stout and masculine.

Aurora Night Stand

Small tables are a great way to work out and experiment with new design ideas (**217**). My progress as a designer can be easily traced in the small tables I have produced over the years. I don't feel every design has to make a bold statement. There is room in the world for simple and quietly pleasing designs.

This small table is an exercise in restraint. There is nothing earth shattering about its design. It does not shout to be heard, nor do I feel it needs to. It is proportioning and the use of negative space that first draws your attention. There are several other details, such as the cloud lift and the Blacker leg indent, that quietly serve for secondary exploration.

The 3/8 inch dowel passing through two small blocks is a pull I have used on many designs over the years, including this nightstand. It is supremely simple, yet it's as functional as it is aesthetically pleasing. I thought myself quite clever for coming up with it. Then some time ago I was sorting through some old papers and came across a poster (**219**) for a James Krenov workshop I had attended many years before. The poster had hung on the wall in my former shop and the only image on it was that of my "clever pull."

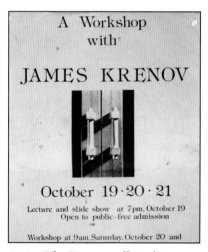

219. *The Krenov pull in this poster was adapted for use in many of Darrell's Greene & Greene inspired designs.*

Aurora Side Chair

While visiting the Greene & Greene archives in Berkeley a few years ago, I came across a photo of a chair from the Ford House. The design was new to me. The back legs splayed out where they meet with the crest rail, giving a slight Asian feel to the chair. This detail interested me.

My purpose in visiting the archives was to search out new (to me) Greene & Greene motifs. I was not looking to copy an original design, but instead to assimilate more Greene & Greene details into my own vocabulary. I had a photocopy of the chair image made, which I took home and studied until I had a strong "feel" for the design. I put the image away, waited a few days, and then started to draw. I relied only upon my memory and my feeling for the detail. The design went through several renderings before I came up with the chair you see here (**221**). The results were far removed from the original design, but I was after the essence of the detail, not a replica. My wife designed and made a quilt using my rendered detail as a repeating pattern. She named the quilt "Berkeley."

I never see my designs as being static. No matter how close to the mark they are, they never seem to precisely match the image in my mind. They are forever a work (or thought) in progress. There is so much yet to explore and refine. It is a process that never ends, nor should it. I have a strong feeling where my designs are headed, but ultimately I want to leave that open. I always feel my best work is in front of me.

220. *Darrell Peart.*

Jeff Zagun

221. *Darrell Peart's Aurora side chair derives its inspiration in part from the Greene & Greene Freeman A. Ford House armchair.*

Chapter 21
Furniture Drawings

The following drawings are presented here as further practical examples of utilizing the Greene & Greene design language. Their purpose is to educate. The drawings are not intended as construction guides, however enough information is given that a resourceful home hobbyist could produce a reasonable facsimile.

Please note: these designs are the property of the author. Reproduction of these designs for commercial purposes is strictly prohibited.

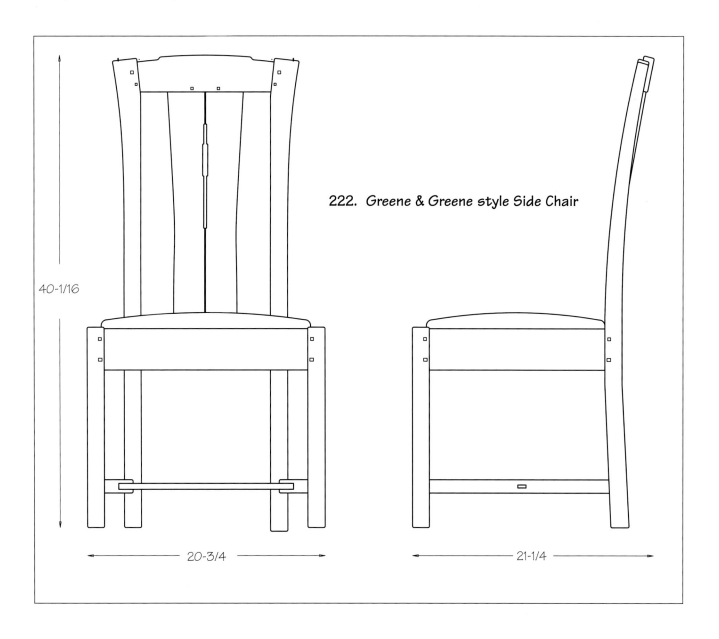

222. Greene & Greene style Side Chair

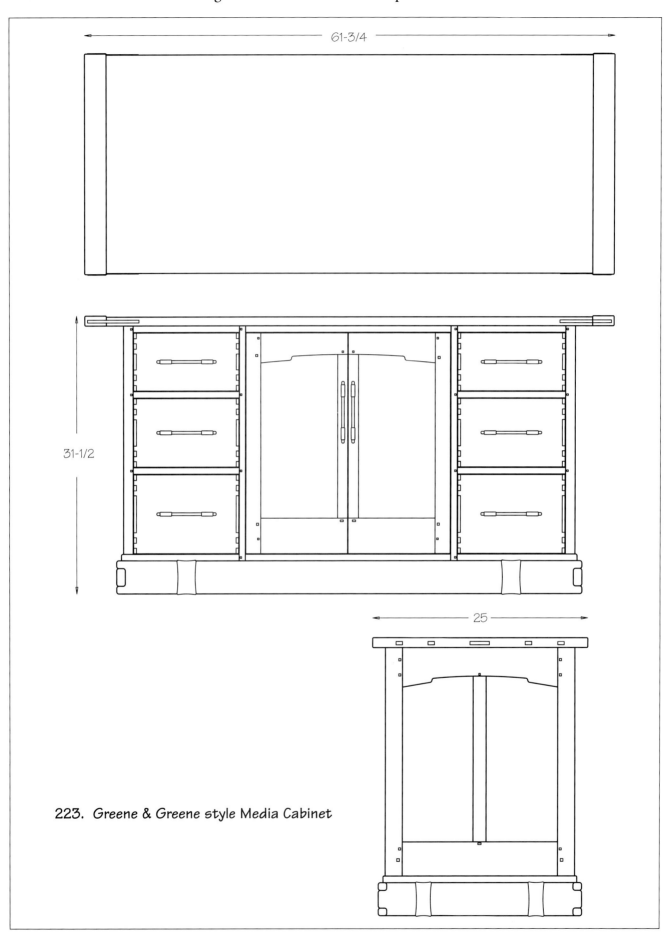

61-3/4

31-1/2

25

223. Greene & Greene style Media Cabinet

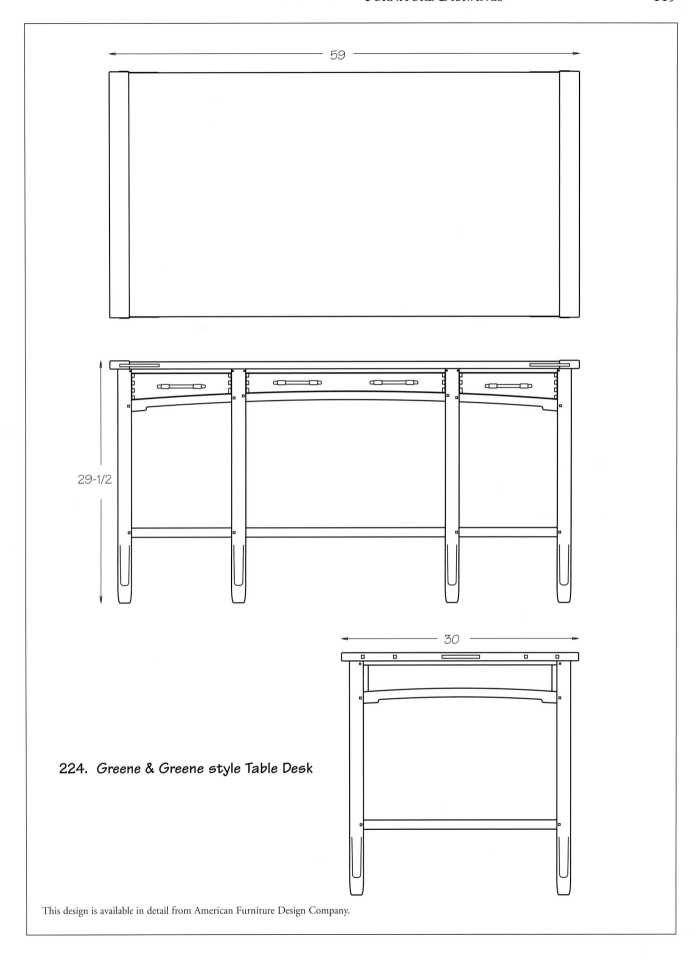

224. Greene & Greene style Table Desk

This design is available in detail from American Furniture Design Company.

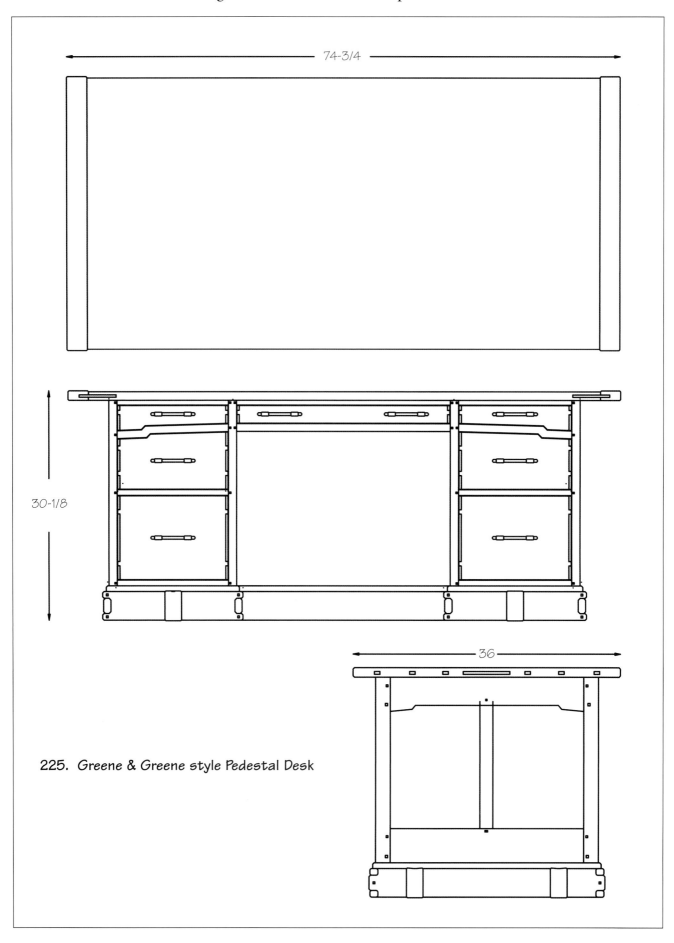

225. Greene & Greene style Pedestal Desk

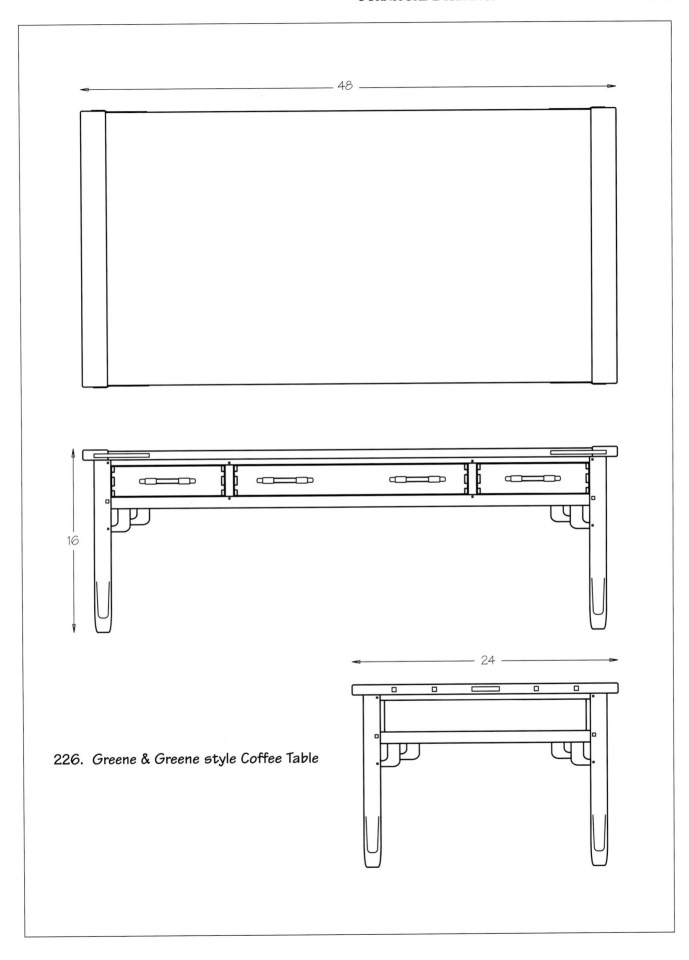

226. Greene & Greene style Coffee Table

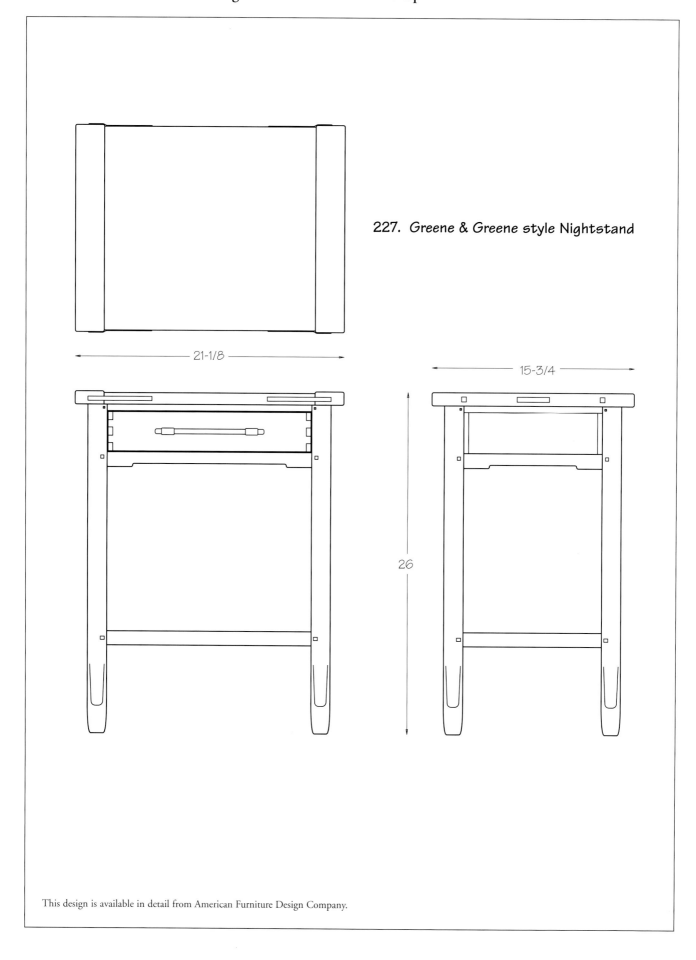

227. Greene & Greene style Nightstand

21-1/8

15-3/4

26

This design is available in detail from American Furniture Design Company.

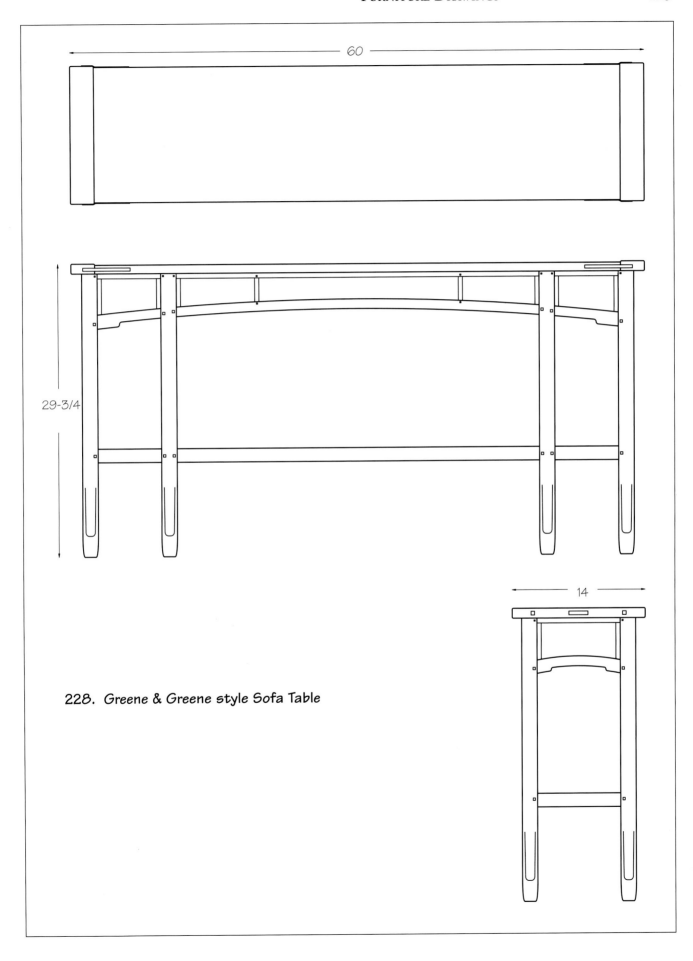

60

29-3/4

14

228. Greene & Greene style Sofa Table

2

Greene & Greene Resources

Archives & Museums

Greene & Greene Virtual Archives:
http://cwis.usc.edu/depth/architecture/greeneandgreene/

Museums / Collected Works of Greene & Greene:
The Huntington Library, Art Collections,
and Botanical Gardens
1151 Oxford Road
San Marino, CA 91108
(626) 405-2100
www.huntington.org

The Los Angeles County Museum of Art
5905 Wilshire Boulevard
Los Angeles, CA 90036
(323) 857-6000 (general information)
(323) 857-0098 (TDD)
www.lacma.org

The Gamble House
4 Westmoreland Place
Pasadena, CA 91103
(626) 793-3334
www.gamblehouse.org/index.html

Furniture Makers

Darrell Peart
Furnituremaker
3419 C Street N.E. #16
Auburn, WA 98002
(425) 277-4070
www.furnituremaker.com

Thomas Stangeland
Artist/Craftsman
312 S. Lucile St.
Seattle, WA 98108
(206) 622-2004
www.artistcraftsman.net/

Arnold d'Epagnier
Mission Evolution
14201 Notley Rd.
Colesville, MD 20904
(301) 384-3201
www.missionevolution.com/

Dale Barnard
The Cabinetmaker
1714 E. Owl Hollow Road
Paoli, IN 47454
(812) 723-3461
www.the-cabinetmaker.com/index.htm

David B. Hellman and Associates
PO Box 526
Watertown, MA 02471
(617) 923-4829
http://members.aol.com/dbhellman/

Jim Ipekjian
504 N. Fair Oaks
Pasadena, CA 91103
(626) 792-5025

Greene & Greene Woodworking Instruction

Connecticut Valley School of Woodworking
249 Spencer St.
Manchester CT 06040
60-647-0303
www.schoolofwoodworking.com

Marc Adams School of Woodworking
5504 E. 500 North
Franklin, IN 46131-7993
(317) 535-4013
www.marcadams.com

William Ng Woodworks School of Fine Woodworking
1345 North Dynamics Street, Suite F
Anaheim, CA 92806
(714) 993-4215
www.wnwoodworks.com/wngschoolmain.htm

Architectural/Homebuilding Services

Tim Andersen
Architect
7726 33rd Avenue N.E.
Seattle, WA 98115-4708
(206) 524-8841
 www.tjandersen.com

Newhaven
Attn: Nick Ericson
PO Box 982
Mukilteo, WA 98275
(425) 493-6800
www.newhavenltd.com

Stained & Leaded Glass

John Hamm
Hamm Glass Studios
(562) 696-2883
www.hammstudios.com

Organizations and Groups

Friends of the Gamble House
4 Westmoreland Place
Pasadena, CA 91103-3593
(626) 793-3334
www.citycent.com/CCC/Pasadena/gambfrnd.htm

Greene & Greene Style Furniture
Yahoo Discussion Group:
http://groups.yahoo.com/group/Greene-style-furniture/

Greene & Greene Woodworking Plans:

American Furniture Design Company
P.O. Box 300100
Escondido, CA 92030
1-760-743-6923
1-760-743-0707 (fax)
http://www.americanfurnituredsgn.com/

Bibliography

Anscombe, Isabelle. *Arts and Crafts Style*, Phaidon Press, Re-issue edition 1996

Bavaro, Joseph J. & Mossman, Thomas L. *The Furniture of Gustav Stickley,* Linden Publishing, 1st Linden Publishing edition 1997

Bosley, Edward R. *Greene & Greene,* Phaidon Press, 2003

Chippendale, Thomas. *Gentleman and Cabinet Maker's Director,* Dover Publications, 3rd edition 1966

Cooke, Edward S. Jr. *Scandinavian Modern Furniture in the Arts and Crafts Period: The Collaboration of the Greenes and the Halls,* The Chipstone Journals, American Furniture 1993

Kaplan, Wendy. *The Art That Is Life: The Art & Crafts Movement in America, 1875-1920,* Bulfinch Press, 1998

Krenov, James. *A Cabinetmaker's Notebook,* Linden Publishing, 2000

Krenov, James. *The Impractical Cabinetmaker,* Linden Publishing, 1st Linden Publishing edition 1999

Krenov, James. *A Cabinetmaker's Notebook,* Van Nostrand Reinhold Co., 1976

Limbert, Charles P. *Limbert's Arts Crafts Furniture,* Turn of the Century Editions, (reprint) 1985

Makinson, Randall L. *Greene and Greene: Architecture as a Fine Art,* Gibbs Smith Publishers, 1977

Makinson, Randall L. *Greene & Greene: Furniture and Related Designs,* Gibbs Smith Publishers, Re-issue edition 1998

Makinson, Randall L. *Greene & Greene: The Passion and the Legacy,* Gibbs Smith Publishers, 1998

Makinson, Randall L. & Heinz, Thomas A. *Greene & Greene: The Blacker House,* Gibbs Smith Publishers, 2000

Marks, Allen. *Greene and Greene: A study in Functional Design,* Fine Woodworking Magazine #12, September 1978 pp. 40 – 45

Smith, Bruce. *Greene & Greene: Masterwork,* Chronicle Books, 1998

Stickley Craftsman Furniture Catalogs – Unabridged Reprints of Two Mission Furniture Catalogs, *Craftsman Furniture Made by Gustav Stickley* and *The Works of L&L.G. Stickley,* Dover Publications, (reprint) 1979

Thomas, Theodore & Jeanette A. *Images of the Gamble House: Masterwork of Greene & Greene*, Balcony Press, 1995

Varnum, William H. *Arts & Crafts Design: A Selected Reprint of Industrial Arts Design,* Gibbs Smith Publishers, Reprint edition 1995

Index

Arts & Crafts Movement, 39, 83

Blacker house, 26, 27, 43, 49, 51, 63, 84, 85
Bed:
    Gamble, 41
    Stangeland, 111
Bench, Stangeland, 110
Bookcase:
    Blacker, 82, 84
    Robinson, 84
Box:
    marquetry, 21
    by Peter Hall, 34
Bracket, 40, 50-57, 61
Breadboard, construction of, 75-76
Bungalow, Ultimate, 10, 26-27, 29
Bush-Bolton house, 62
Bush & Gamble, 84

Cabinet:
    Blacker entry hall, 49
    Bush curio, 61
    d'Epagnier, 104
    drawing of, 118
    Thorsen living room, 58
Chair:
    Blacker, 27, 43, 51
    Fleishhacker, 33
    drawing of, 117
    Gamble, 10
    Peart, Aurora, 116
    Pratt, 29
    Stangeland, 108-109
    Thorsen, 9, 28, 30, 63, 64
    Tichenor, 17
Chippendale, Thomas, 27, 43
Chiffonier, Gamble, 24, 70, 92
Chisel, 64

Cloud lift detail, 26, 29, 40, 58-60
Culbertson house, 31, 50, 51
Cygnaeus, Uno, 25

Dart, Emeline, 15
d'Epagnier, Arnold, 104-107
Desk:
    d'Epagnier, 107
    James, 32
    Peart, 112
    Tichenor, 17
Detail, cloud lift, 29, 40, 59
Dowels, boring for, 54-55
Drawer, 70, 83, 84, 91-97
Dye, for wood, 98-99

Escutcheon, wooden, 83

Fleishhacker house, 34
Foot, claw & ball, 43
Ford house, 23
Frieze, by John Hall, 20
Furniture, Chinese, 43, 63
Furniture, contemporary:
    Barnard, Dale, 124
    d'Epagnier, Arnold, 104, 105-108, 124
    Hellman, David B, 124
    Ipekjian, Jim, 124
    Peart, Darrell, 112-116, 124
    Stangeland, Thomas, 109-111, 124
Furniture, Greene & Greene:
    Blacker, 26, 27, 82, 84, 109, 113
    Bush, 61
    complexity of, 39
    Fleishhacker, 32, 34
    Gamble, 70, 72
    James, 32

rarity of, 8, 39
Reeve, 25
Robinson, 26
X-rays of, 9, 27, 51

Gamble house, 26, 72, 84, 124
Gibbs-Smith, publishers, 103
Golden rectangle, 103
Gould house, 15
Greene & Greene:
    comparison with Stickley, 37-38
    early furniture of, 15-17
    hardware of, 83
    joinery of, 28
    largest commission of, 34
Greene, Charles Sumner:
    aesthetics of, 9
    Asian influences, 16, 28, 40
    birth of, 12
    brackets by, 51
    breadboard by, 74-75
    cloud lift by, 59
    design process of, 26, 28, 41
    early career of, 14
    ebony plugs by, 63
    ebony spline by, 79
    education of, 13
    hardware by, 83
    late career of, 31-32
    leg detail by, 43
    move to Carmel, 31
    relief detail by, 71
    unbuilt furniture of, 32
    vision of, 11, 14, 27
Greene, Henry Mather:
    birth of, 12
    education of, 13
    early career of, 14
    the engineer, 15

(INDEX continued)

Greene, Lelia Ariane, 12-13
Greene, Thomas Sumner, 12-13

Hall, Donald, 20
Hall, John:
    birth of, 18
    carving by, 20-21
    early mirror by, 19
    sensitivity of, 21
Hall, Peter:
    abilities of, 28-29
    birth of, 18
    meets the Greenes, 22
    sensibilities of, 21
    workshop of, 22, 25, 34
Hall, John and Peter:
    adjustable shelves by, 83
    Sloyd training of, 23
    Swedish employees of, 26, 30
Houses, Greene & Greene:
    Bush/Bolton, 62
    Blacker, 26, 27, 43, 49, 51, 63,
        84, 85
    Culbertson, 31, 50, 51
    Fleishhacker (Green Gables), 34
    Ford, 23
    Gamble, 26, 72, 84, 124
    Gould, 15
    James, 31-32
    Merwin, 23
    Oakholm, 15
    Pratt, 29
    Reeve, 16, 62
    Robinson, 23, 26, 62, 71-72, 83
    Thorsen, 26, 29, 72-73, 83, 84
    Tichenor, 17
    White, 22

Inlay:
    Black-Eyed Susan, 106
    bolection, 42

James house, 32
Jig:
    for ebony plug, 66
    for leg indent, 44-45
    for Blacker pull, 85-86
Joinery, faux, 9, 28

Jonasson, Jon, 18

Krenov, James, 113, 115

Larsdotter, Sissa, 18
Leg:
    indent of, 48
    router jig for, 44-45
    treatment of, 43
Limbert, Charles, 59

Marks, Alan, 113, 126
Merwin house, 23
Miller, George A., poem by, 20
Mirror:
    by d'Epagnier, 105
    by Halls, 19, 22
Morris, William, 35
Mortise, 64

Nelson, Jennie, 18
Nightstand, Peart Aurora, 114, 122

Oakholm, 15

Pasadena, move to, 13, 14-17
Peart, Darrel, 112-116
Plug, ebony, 4, 45, 46, 62, 63, 67-
    70, 77
Pratt house, 29
Pull, ebony, 84

Rail, crest, 30
Reeve house, 16, 62
Richardson, H.H., 13, 41
Roberts, Lida Alice, 21
Robinson house, 23, 26, 62, 72, 83
Router, 45-46, 77, 79, 87
Ruskin, John, 35

Screen, Tichenor, 16
Shelf, adjustable, 83
Sideboard:
    d'Epagnier, 107
    Stickley, 38
    Thorsen, 40-41, 82, 84
Sloyd system, 16, 26, 82
Solomon, Otto, 25
Spline, ebony, 74, 77, 78, 79-80

Stangeland, Thomas, 108-111
Stickley, Gustav, 15, 16, 26, 28, 35-
    39, 59, 71, 74, 83, 102
Stretcher, 29

Table:
    Bolton-Bush, 62
    drawing of, 119, 120, 121, 123
    Fleishhacker, 33
    Gamble, 39
    James, 32
    Peart Aurora, 112
    Stangeland, 108, 110, 111
    Stickley, 36, 38
    Thorsen, 11
    wedding gift, 14
    White sisters, 15
Template:
    for brackets, 52
    for cloud lift, 59
    for ebony spline, 79-80
    for knuckle, 47
Thorsen house, 26, 29, 72, 83, 84
Tichenor, Adelaide, 16
Tichenor house, 17
Tsuba, 4, 40-41, 102

Varnum, William H., 103

White house, 22